DRIFTING IN THE WAKE

The Unusual and Remarkable Life of Orville Wright Jr.

ORVILLE WRIGHT

WRIGHT PUBLISHING
COMPANY

Wright Publishing Company

ISBN: 978-0-578-22083-3

Library of Congress Control Number: 2019911076

Cover Photo © 2019 John Mullen. All rights reserved - used with permission.

PRINTED IN THE UNITED STATES OF AMERICA

Acknowledgments

I believe editing someone else's memoirs has to rank in the top 10 most thankless tasks requested of friends. To authors with fragile egos, any suggestions may be interpreted as harsh and personal criticism. Having survived 10 years growing up in a children's home, as well as a humiliating year as a plebe at the Naval Academy, all semblance of sensitivity was removed.

With that in mind, I want to thank several friends that did a superb job of correcting my draft copy and making it more interesting and readable. They are Linda Brisson from Ithaca, NY, Karen Bernardo from Vestal, NY, Wally Weller, an old shipmate from Anacortes, WA and of course, my wife and counselor, Carolyn Wright. I am truly indebted.

In addition, I would like to acknowledge the two outstanding photographers who contributed to the superb cover. The head shot is attributed to Stephen Appel of Vestal, NY and the Navy helicopter is by John Mullen of Endicott, NY. Also, a huge thank you to indexer extraordinaire, Judy Kip of Owego, NY.

Table of Contents

Preface

Artificial Intelligence is no match for Natural Stupidity.

EVEN THOUGH MY youngest son John had tried on several occasions to convince me to write my memoirs, I had given the idea short shrift until my retirement trip back to the United States on the QE 2. The theme for the crossing was British novelists. There were four or five distinguished authors on board. During one question-and-answer session, a questioner asked about the pros and cons of writing one's life history. William Horwood was so enthusiastic about individuals penning their memoirs that it convinced me to make the effort. "Nothing you do in life will be more important to your children and their children than to put pen to paper and record the relevant happenings in your life," he said.

After the decision to publish was made, the outline was the next hurdle. Since my life had defined segments, it seemed logical to map out the chapters by those segments. The problem with that approach is that certain philosophies of living, such as the telling lies to your children every day and "planned disappointment programs," have no specified chapter.

The final decision was to determine what adventures were worth sharing and which would simply bore the reader. Since my wife will testify that my memory is not infallible, some of the specific details may not meet the rigid requirements necessary in a court of law with regard to establishing truth. But, to the best of my knowledge, every event I record here either I witnessed or heard about from a reliable source.

CHAPTER 1

The First Seven Years

Learn to be sincere, even if you have to fake it.

I AM NOT sure where my sense of destiny originated. Perhaps it was as simple as the fact that I never recalled my father saying a critical comment to me or about me in my entire life. That is a fairly unusual situation for a second child (first son) born in the 1930s and sent to a children's home at the age of seven. In any case, I have always been convinced that some divine power had selected me to be the recipient of good luck and fortune throughout my life.

My grandfather, John C. Wright, was born in October 1880 in Circleville, Ohio. He was a cook on the railroad for most of his life and was active in union affairs. He married Olive Maley about the turn of the century and within three years, had two sons. They lived on Chicago's South Side where they raised their family in typical God fearing, Roman Catholic fashion. Their eldest son was named John Michael and he was born on May 12, 1902. Orville John, my father, was born 365 days later, a curious coincidence. On December 17, 1903, the Wright brothers successfully flew their bi-wing plane at Kitty Hawk, North Carolina. (Although there was no family relationship, the opportunity for my father, years later, to name his sons Orville and Wilbur was just too delicious for him to pass up.)

John C. and Olive later moved to Oak Park, Illinois, a nice suburb of Chicago. He continued working on the railroad while she ran a small restaurant called Mrs. Wright's Dining Room. Olive suffered a stroke in 1950 and died at the age of 68. John lived an additional 13 years but he seemed like a lost soul without his wife to keep him on the straight and narrow.

John M., Dad's brother, ended up in jail as a teenager. He committed suicide while incarcerated. No one in the family ever spoke about the event. Keeping family secrets was not unusual 100 years ago but it was quite a shock to me when I found out about it after Dad had died and I was doing research for this book. I thought it very strange that he never disclosed the fact that he was not an only child.

When war was declared in 1917, Dad was too young to enlist in the armed forces. As soon as he turned 15 in May 1918, he added a year to his age in a clumsy forgery to his birth certificate. He enlisted in the Navy as a hospital apprentice. Since Dad could not stand the sight of blood, it is curious that the U.S. Navy thought it could turn him into a corpsman. It is not clear whether his mother came to boot camp and retrieved him or he just went AWOL (absent without leave). In any case, the Navy classified him as a deserter and scheduled a general court martial for young Orville John. When the court realized he was too young to enlist, it gave him an undesirable discharge.

After graduating from high school, Dad took an apprenticeship as a shirt-cutter, which started him on a career in men's clothing that would last until 1969, when he retired from civil service as a clothing inspector and moved to Florida to live his lifelong dream. His job in retailing took him to Philadelphia, Detroit, Kansas City, and New York City.

He rose as high as managing The Custom Shop in Wanamaker's department store in Philadelphia but resigned when the company merged three departments into two. As the junior manager, he was to be reassigned into a less prestigious role in the store.

Dad's first marriage was to a young society woman in Chicago in 1926. But they were so incompatible they were separated within twelve months. It didn't take a professional marriage counselor to conclude that a shirt cutter from the South Side wouldn't find happiness marrying into an affluent family that valued higher education, the arts, fashion shows and opera. That starter marriage cost him a weekly alimony of $15. Within two years he had courted and married Alva Dorris, a young woman from Ranger, Texas, and had three children from 1931 (Jean) until 1935 (Wilbur). I was born in January of 1934 in Philadelphia in the middle of the Great Depression.

My mother, Alva, was the third youngest among 12 siblings and was born about 1910. The oldest Dorris girl was Xia, who traveled to New Mexico in a covered wagon. Another sister, Wilda, lived in Dallas for many years and was the quintessential Texan, larger than life, loud, with a surplus of humorous stories. A younger brother, Cone, was a master sergeant in the Army. Alva and her younger sister Helen left the ranch after high school to pursue a career in the big city. The Dorris sisters were personable and attractive and they were both soon married. But, in 1941 Alva was diagnosed with cancer. It was decided that she would return to Texas for rehabilitation. She succumbed to the disease in early 1942. None of the children attended the funeral and no contact was made with my mother's side of the family until many years later. Dad remained persona non grata with most of the Dorris clan for the rest of his life. I, however, established a close relationship with Aunt Helen Brewer as an adult and maintained a lasting friendship with all four of her children, John, Peter, David and Susan.

Dad subsequently met a young second generation Armenian named Shacki Karakashian at a local bowling alley. He married her in June 1944. Shacki was unaware that he was the father of three children until sometime after the wedding ceremony took place in Toledo, Ohio. Shacki was the youngest of four children and was raised on a tight leash by her parents, who had emigrated from Armenia. Her older brother Paul was killed in World War II. A second brother, Nubar, was a successful ophthalmologist in the Philadelphia area and her older sister, Virginia, a dress designer and the mother of two girls. Shacki worked as a hairdresser as she followed dad from Detroit to

St. Paul, Minnesota, to Ann Arbor, Michigan, to Philadelphia, to New York City, and back to Philly.

My memories of early childhood consisted of a vacation in the Pocono Mountains, where I caught the mumps and spent the week in a chaise lounge recovering. Another remembrance was an incident where Brother Will was playing with matches when he was four and the mattress caught fire in the bedroom upstairs. I recall my mother shouting, 'Fire' and someone, perhaps from the fire department, pushing the smoldering mattress out the window. The only other memorable experience for me that comes to mind was one night when my father came home from work and offered me a piece of Wrigley's gum. On extracting a stick, a spring-loaded 'snapper' caught my thumb, which resulted in a tearful run to mom.

When it became apparent that the family was breaking up in the summer of 1941, Dad's parents volunteered to take care of Jean but they were unable to take all three grandchildren. After spending the summer at a New Jersey boarding house, six year old Wilbur and Orville Jr., age seven years and eight months, were sent off to Tabor Home for Children in Doylestown, Pennsylvania.

CHAPTER 2

Tabor Home for Children

Life isn't fair, but it's still good.

MOST PEOPLE ENVISION that childrens' homes or orphanages are quite similar to the one to which Dickens' Oliver Twist was condemned. Or, perhaps like the one housing Little Orphan Annie or Father Flanagan's Boys' Town in Nebraska. In truth, there is probably as wide a variation among institutions housing children as there is among two parent households in the country. Any generalization such as 'foster homes are good, institutions are bad' is as wrong as often as it is right.

It is fair to say that any child institutionalized at a young age will end up with a set of values and a personality different than if he had been raised by a set of loving and supportive parents. But, as far as a predictor for success in life, one could make a convincing argument favoring the parentless child.

Tabor Home for Children was located on 99 acres of Bucks County farmland, one mile south of Doylestown, Pennsylvania. It was founded in Philadelphia when Mrs. Emma Chidester of the Tabor Evangelical Lutheran Church offered her Cheltenham residence as a home for destitute children. It moved out of the city in 1913. It was sponsored and supported by the Lutheran Church and staffed by deaconesses out of the Philadelphia motherhouse. It also received

Pennsylvania state financial aid. Application for acceptance to Tabor was made through the courts. The vast majority of the children accepted in the 1940s and 1950s were from broken homes with neither parent in a position to financially support their child in their home. A small number of orphans were assigned to Tabor by the courts, but most of the children in residence had at least one parent living. It should be remembered that there were no social service organizations to assist families having financial or structural difficulties.

The physical layout of the Home was impressive. The starting point was the massive 18-foot high black gate with the words Tabor Home for Children adorned in gold paint across the top. A winding road surrounded by green lawns and trees ended in a circular drive at the administrative building, the original Fretz mansion. On the right side of the road a softball field was situated with a homemade backstop. Although constructed of chicken wire, it kept passed balls from rolling into the woods. There was a swimming pool that was used during the summer months. Every 45 days the algae would coat the sides with a green slime. The pool would then be emptied and the sides cleaned. The two and one-half-inch water pipe would deliver clean swimming water for another month and a half. Watching the pool refill seemed to take an eternity. In fact, it took almost three days. The water was frigid when the pool reopened but the sun and childrens' body heat soon rectified that.

The rest of the acreage consisted of agricultural fields that produced potatoes, hay, wheat and corn. In addition there was a truck patch that was located adjacent to the main gate, right on Route 611. A variety of vegetables were grown and cultivated in this humongous garden. Tabor kids all developed skills in weeding that would benefit them throughout their lifetime. Across the highway were the barn, additional fields, and the tenant farmer's house. The remainder of the land was covered with wooded terrain, which the boys utilized as a huge battleground. The country was at war and simulated combat was a favorite pastime for the youngsters living there.

The staff consisted of five full time Lutheran sisters augmented by several part-time assistants in the summer months when all 80 children were not in school. The children attended Doylestown Township Consolidated School, a half mile down the road in Edison, Pennsylvania. Following graduation from the eighth grade, students enrolled in Doylestown High School. The Home did not have a good high school graduation record in the late 1930s, particularly among the girls. Sometimes a 16-year-old girl was requested to pack up and leave following minor violations of house rules, such as sassing a Sister.

Arriving at Tabor in September of 1941 was traumatic for both Wilbur (Will) and me, but children are quite adaptable. They accept situations over which they have minimal say. The girls' house, in the final stages of completion, was an impressive two story stone dormitory that housed 40 girls from ages five to 17. It contained a huge dining room, a restaurant sized kitchen and locked storerooms packed with canned fruits, vegetables, and juices. These rooms were targeted by bands of hungry boys, intent on appropriating number 10 cans of fruit such as peaches, pears, or apricots. It also housed an auditorium in the basement, which was used for meetings, religious services, and to stage plays and musicals. On the second floor were about 12 rooms, each accommodating four girls to a room. The second floor was off limits to boys, but occasionally boys would sneak into the girls' rooms at night.

The boys' house was a cut granite structure, converted from an old carriage house in about 1917, and consisting of two large dormitory style bedrooms on the second floor. The front room housed the younger children up to age 12 or 13. The back room was where the big guys lived. Each child in the front room owned a 12 inch by 12 inch cubbyhole where his clothes were stored, plus a hook to hang up the remaining clothes. It was similar to a 'one on, one off and one in the wash' scenario. Boys also stored their baseball gloves, bats, balls, and other sports gear in a seat-type chest on the ground floor. Laundry was done on Mondays and kids were responsible for getting their dirty clothes in the laundry bag by Sunday night.

Every child was assigned a number, which was stitched on each piece of clothing to show ownership. My number was 111 and I was quite proud of it. Owning anything was not important to Tabor kids, as they commonly swapped clothes and sporting equipment. The ground floor contained a glassed-in rectangular porch, where assigned storage boxes were located. Each child had their own locked box. A large playroom with hardwood floors was also located on the same floor and one passed through a smaller playroom en route to the downstairs boys' bathroom. The bathroom consisted of about four stalls for toilets in a big shower room. A weekly shower was prescribed but no one was fanatical about enforcing it. The third floor was unused during normal conditions, but was occasionally used as a 'sick room' in the event any of the children caught any communicable diseases. The second floor of the laundry room was also used as an isolation ward.

The third major building was the original girls' house where we ate meals before 1942. It was converted into a study hall, main office, and residence of the head mistress. It was where the first television set was located after Sara Duckworth, one of the Home girls, won a black and white set in a contest. One of my early memories of mealtime was looking forward to breakfast. The little kids were given two pieces of bread spread with molasses, which soaked into the bread. Everyone loved it and it was used as a medium of exchange. "I'll give you three pieces of molasses bread if you will..." These were uncomplicated times.

Sister Lena Beideck was the head mistress from about 1913 until Sister Wilma Loehrig replaced her in 1942. Sister Lena was loved by most of the kids, but she did not run a tight ship. Tabor's reputation was less than stellar for producing kids that were not high school dropouts. So the children tended to raise themselves with minimal guidance from positive role models.

With the arrival of Sister Wilma, the Home became a lot more structured. No longer was it sufficient to 'meet standards.' Kids with talent were encouraged to strive for success in life. This was expected in academics as well as athletics. From the time she arrived in 1942 until she retired in 1971, it was assumed all Tabor kids would graduate from high school and apply for college or join the armed forces. It became unacceptable to drop out of school at age 16 and start working.

Life at Tabor was about acquiring survival skills as rapidly as possible so that wise decisions could be made with minimal discomfort. A pecking order was quickly established so you knew whom you could beat up and who could beat you up. But actually, there was not much fighting once the ground rules were established. Acts of kindness regarding new arrivals at the home were few and far between. Your moniker was 'new kid.' That was how everyone addressed the novice. It could be weeks or months before others referred to you by your name. This probation period lasted until the next 'new kid' arrived.

One of my earliest and most traumatic experiences occurred early in the school year of 1941, shortly after arriving at Tabor. Changing schools in the third grade should have been seamless since most material should have been covered in the first two years. But the Upper Darby school in suburban Philadelphia introduced neither cursive writing nor long division before school year three. I was the only child in grade three who was printing during writing class. I did not have a clue how to solve long division problems. My solution to the latter was to feign a stomachache when the class was asked to do division. One day after being sent home, I found myself transported to a hospital in Philadelphia where they relieved me of my appendix. Even as a seven-year-old, I realized that some seemingly cunning solutions had unintended consequences.

Tabor Home residents and cast of characters:

- Jake Highton: One of the positive role models at Tabor. Sports fanatic and journalism major at Penn State. First Tabor kid who attended college. Wrote sports for the *Doylestown Intelligencer*. Pretty good side arm baseball pitcher, high jumper, and starting end on the high school football team.

9

- Don "Fats" Allison: Colleague of Jake and one of the back-room guys. Came to Tabor as a slightly overweight child, and although possessing a normal build, carried the disparaging nickname. Good athlete and catcher on the baseball team.
- Brother Will: Natural athlete and the original 'no sweat' teenager. His philosophy in life was to exert only enough effort to skim over the bar. He always dated the prettiest girls in school and was everyone's favorite. He was just a couple of names from the 'anchorman' when he graduated from the Naval Academy in 1958.
- Albert McGettigan: Pint sized kid with a great singing voice.
- Don 'Stilts' Fritz: One of the true orphans at Tabor. He was so obsessed with sports from the time he showed up in 1945 as a tall nine-year-old that someone remarked that he looked as if he were walking on stilts. The moniker stuck for about 10 years. Later he was named to the Central Bucks High School Hall of Fame as a four sport athlete. He was a close friend of my Brother Will.
- Walt Evans: The only child of a mother who had emigrated from Germany. He never lived down the fact that his mother commented that one day she would say, "Pack up Walter, we're going back to Germany." Anything associating a child with either Japan or Germany during World War II was the kiss of death. Walt was bright and had an excellent singing voice.
- The Hoppe boys: Family of three boys who were often involved in any mischievous adventures at the home. Joe was the eldest and worked at the barn, milking the cows. Carl was athletic and disciplined and loved playing combat in the woods. (Jake Highton still has a scar on his hand from being stabbed by Carl with a wooden bayonet when playing commandos in the Tabor woods.) Bobby 'Toad' Hoppe was the baby and became a foreign missionary in later life.

- The Maloney sisters, Dorothea and Eleanor: Dotty was in my class throughout high school. She was always a huge fan of mine. She was a cheerleader in high school and among the most popular students in the class. Dotty was not one of Sister Wilma's favorites primarily because the sister favored boys over the girls. Eleanor was one year younger and was often in hot water with the staff because she exhibited such teenager characteristics as sullenness and flippancy.

To capture the essence of 10 years of life at Tabor in a single chapter was difficult since it involved tears, great joy, laughter, cruelty, enduring friendship, fights, and a realization that life was not fair. Tears were a common sight among the younger children as they tried to establish their position among their peers while remaining on the right side of the authorities. Great joy was in shorter supply but was supplied by athletic success. Laughter was ubiquitous since much of the time we were creating our own games of simulated combat and athletic competition. The older boys sometimes inflicted cruel treatment on the younger ones, such as unprovoked punching or snatching a favorite possession, although there were unspoken rules of engagement. Bullying to instill fear was not practiced since there was a sense of symbiosis among all the children. Despite some amount of internal disagreement, anytime Tabor kids came under fire, they would have the backing of every other Home kid. That sense of loyalty creates enduring friendships. It did not take long to catch on about life's inequalities and that you had better play the cards you were dealt. Public school teachers, parents of friends, and newspaper journalists reinforced one's position in the class system. Virtually every published article about a Tabor child or alumnus would always have the theme, 'Tabor kid makes good.'

The older a child was when he began his tenure at the Home, the less lasting impact it tended to have on his psyche and sense of self worth. All children raised at Tabor suffered basic feelings of insecurity. They developed mechanisms to cope with being powerless in an adult world. But for those starting under the age of six, it seemed particularly traumatic. A common trait exhibited by many of the kids was a tendency to admit a failure soon after meeting someone for the first time. Failing a test or being 'left back' in school might be disclosed quickly. This not only disarmed the other person but it was a protection against criticism.

The Edison Elementary School, attended by Tabor children, consisted of grades one through eight with the top three grades sharing one large dividable room. The principal and eighth grade teacher was a pudgy Dutchman by the name of Paul Kutz. His wife taught the sixth and seventh grades. She was a delightful and caring person. Paul was an insensitive bully who had little compassion or concern about students who came from underprivileged families, which included all Tabor kids. His technique was leadership by humiliation. A student by the name of John Palermo was one grade ahead of me. Paul would periodically ask John the same question in class, "What is the name of the principal city of Sicily, Palermo?" Poor John would always say he didn't know. The class repeatedly found it amusing.

The American Legion awarded a medal to the eighth grade student who was voted by the class to have contributed the most during the school year. Traditionally, the president of the class was given the honor, which happened to be me in 1947. Just before graduation, Kutz conducted the voting with these preliminary remarks, "It is time to vote for the Legion award which will be presented during the commencement ceremonies. Vote for the person who has contributed the most for the class. I don't want you to vote for a deadhead like Wright." I had no idea why he thought I was a loser. The class followed his suggestion and voted for Bob Ott. He and Dorothea Maloney accepted the awards at graduation.

Bucks County sponsored standardized testing for all eighth graders in math, reading, spelling, and English. One of the high school girls at Tabor, Josie Montieth, was working in the county office. One of her tasks was to grade and record scores of the various tests. She told me that I had scored the highest grade in both English and arithmetic.

At the eighth grade graduation ceremony the $2.50 stipend for the highest average in arithmetic was awarded to me but the $5 English award was presented to Rosalind Case, a classmate. The school might have had a policy of not giving multiple awards, but it seemed quite unjust to me. The sad part of the story was that I wasn't surprised at the obvious bias on the part of the principal. I didn't take it personally. He felt that way about all the Tabor kids. I learned at an early age that life was not necessarily fair.

It is ironic that after several of his "doomed students" from Tabor were lauded for their athletic and scholastic achievements, Principal Kutz bragged to colleagues about 'his boys' and the role he played in their development. The Edison elementary school was named for him following his retirement. His obituary lionized him as a giant among Pennsylvania educators. But to us Tabor kids he was no giant.

It has been said that most people will die with the ability to recall only 10 memorable days in their lifetime. I could accept that observation only if large numbers of elderly people with advanced stages of Alzheimer's disease were included in the study. Any former Tabor kid can come up with 10 memorable childhood days in about 10 minutes time. And they do so with appropriate levels of humor, pathos and nostalgia. Here are just a few I remember:

A farmer who was a former Tabor resident, Harry "Boog" Burmeister, carried out the day to day management of the dairy and truck farm. He recruited one willing victim among the crop of teenage boys to assist in the milking of the cows and the cleaning out the stables. The onus of finding a replacement was placed on the current victim in the event he wanted relief from his job. It was always unclear to me why anyone would volunteer for such an onerous job. But Fats Allison, Joe Hoppe, and Don Fritz were the designated assistants during the 1940s. They seemed quite happy with their elevated status in life.

While the majority of the children had to get permission from Sister Wilma to leave the grounds for any extracurricular activity, the 'barn boys' negotiated directly with the head farmer. Chores such as sweeping the pavements and driveways, hand mowing the acres of grass, making hay, shucking corn in the autumn, weeding the rows of vegetables, picking up potatoes, and threshing wheat in the summer had to be completed in a satisfactory manner before leisure activities were permitted. It was a pragmatic control mechanism that worked effectively.

One of the early stories involved Jake Highton and Fats Allison taking the pickup truck for a joyride before either of them had their license to drive. 'Boog' had vacated the premises temporarily and carelessly failed to remove the ignition keys. With Jake driving, the adventure was proceeding nicely until a narrow bridge was encountered with a car coming in the other direction at fairly high speed. It was reported that Jake just shut his eyes and prayed there was room. Apparently there was since both perpetrators returned safely and no one was the wiser about the incident. Events of this potential life-threatening magnitude were quite unusual in all the years I lived at Tabor.

World War II started in December of 1941, several months after Will and I came to Tabor. The war had a significant impact on many of the childrens' day to day activities. Rationing of food and gasoline was a way of life. Several Dutch sailors spent a few weeks in rehabilitation at Tabor after their submarine was sunk off the Eastern coastline. Everyone was fascinated with the war and events both in Europe and the Pacific theaters. They were followed with great interest. In mid 1942 when the Germans were trying to push the Russians off the Crimean peninsula into the Black Sea, Jake Highton and I were sitting on the rear seat on Tabor's bus returning from church one Sunday. We were pushing each other off the seat (Crimean peninsula) amid loud cries of victory. The bus driver, Joe Moskavitz, in his mid twenties, was the temporary assistant farmer. Halfway home Sister Wilma had Joe stop the bus. She banished both the German and Russian gladiators from the vehicle because our excessive noise was 'upsetting Joe.' The two war weary combatants trudged the remaining half a mile home.

Good judgment was not always the order of the day. I recall that several 10 to 12-year-old boys decided to pick teams and have a dart fight. The contest ended early when Carl Hoppe got hit in the eye with a thrown dart. He lost most of his vision and all future metal dart games involving live targets were banned.

On the northern border of Tabor Home was the Coulton residence. The youngest child, named Bruce (now deceased), was a classmate at Edison. He lived in a two story green house with an older brother George, and they kept a 10 acre truck farm and a small apple orchard. They had little use for Tabor kids and this was quite obvious in their demeanor. Perhaps there was some justification for their malevolent behavior toward the next-door thieves that occasionally stole their apples. In any case, there was no love lost regarding the Coultons.

A relatively benign weapon that was commonly used by the young boys to shoot at birds and squirrels was a foot-long piece of inner tube attached by two strings to a small pouch, which held the stones. It was called a 'slappie' and the range of the small rocks varied from about 20 to 75 yards. One morning Albert McGettigan and I decided to experiment with a two man slappie that would have a range of 100 yards and hurl a two pound rock. The basic flaw in the concept was that a coordinated maneuver involving the rapid lowering of the thumb was necessary in order to preclude the accelerating rock from striking the forward holder's thumb. After the initial failure and the icing down of Al's swollen thumb, we went back to the drawing board and devised a giant sling shot, which minimized the probability of self-injury. After cutting down a small sapling which formed a large Y, we tied two bungee-like rubber strips to the small tree, creating a slingshot about six feet high and capable of hurling a fist sized rock several hundred yards. It did not occur to us that if this rock struck someone in the head, it could be lethal. We took our invention up to the far side of the woods and spotted George Coulton cultivating his field about 200 yards away. We aimed our contraption and watched as our rock followed a 45 degree arc, striking the shocked target in the leg.

Since we were on the edge of the woods, we immediately abandoned our homemade weapon and high tailed it back to safer ground.

The now limping and furious neighbor went directly to Sister Wilma to report the incident and seek redress for the dastardly deed. She asked the complainant to identify the culprits so she could take action. "I don't know. All Tabor kids look alike," was George's response. Since he was unable to shed any light on the identification of the possible perpetrators, she dismissed him with a shrug of her shoulders. This was not one of my finest hours – the potential injuries it could have inflicted on an innocent neighbor could not be justified.

On more than one occasion we would not be so fortunate in escaping detection for deeds most foul. The punishment that was most often meted out was standing on the stage in the dining room while everyone else ate dinner. I recall a specific incident where several of us were caught stealing pumpkins and our punishment was to consume the raw pumpkin on the stage in front of all the kids. The audience thought it was great fun.

Singing was always encouraged at Tabor. If you could carry a tune, it was expected you would sing in the Lutheran Church choir. The choir would practice once a week to prepare for the Sunday morning service. Both Will and I along with two or three other heavenly voices would walk the mile or so to the Lutheran Church on Thursday evenings and prepare for the weekend festivities. Walter Evans and Albert McGettigan were colleagues with quite good singing voices. The problem with Evansie was that he couldn't do anything right. I often punched him on the arm to express my displeasure at his being a quintessential 'screw up,' which I felt reflected badly on all Tabor kids. He seemed helpless to change, however. One night as we returned home from choir practice, God smiled on us as we passed the Lewis Atlantic gas station south of town. The owner had forgotten to lock the outdoor cooler and it was full of soft drinks. We all helped ourselves and consumed them as we proceeded on foot down Route 611, which connected Doylestown and Tabor, congratulating ourselves on our good fortune. Unbeknown to us, a neighbor had seen us and reported the theft to the local police, who responded within several minutes.

As their squad car pulled up, the lead law enforcement officer inquired as to whether we had seen anyone taking bottles of soda pop from the gas station. As you might expect, we denied it, aghast that he would accuse us of such a heinous crime. After all, we were members of the church choir and had been singing the Lord's praises just minutes before.

The sound of Evansie's half consumed soft drink bottle breaking on the macadam highway interrupted our plea of innocence and acted like a starter's pistol at a track meet. As we fled toward the inviting cornfield just a hundred yards away, we all denounced the day Walter Evans showed up at Tabor. The cops tried to scare us out of the darkened cornfield with a loud threat of shooting into the field. We could barely contain our laughter. All members of the angelic choir crept home after Doylestown's finest gave up and drove away.

Of all of the holidays, Christmas meant the most to Tabor kids. All the local charities seemed to band together and contribute gifts, money, clothes, and candy to the Home. Every year the Emergency Police gave each individual a box containing an orange surrounded with hard candy. We loved it since most of the year there was a distinct shortage of luxuries that most children take for granted.

Friehofer's bakery would deliver bread and rolls to Tabor on a daily basis. The driver would sell day old pastries to the kids for five cents. Purchasing six sticky buns for a nickel was the closest thing to Nirvana that most of the children ever experienced. The excitement that a nickel in your pocket could command, while waiting for the bakery truck, was unbelievable.

On their 12th birthday, Tabor boys joined the Boy Scouts. Nearly every Tabor boy was a member of the Edison troop. It meant weekly meetings, summer camp, projects to attain merit badges and occasional community events. One learned a variety of skills that increased your confidence to survive in the woods. Jake Highton attained the rank of Eagle Scout but most of the rest of us dropped out of the program before we earned the required merit badges. I was two merit badges short of Eagle before high school sports took priority.

Nevertheless, I retain fond memories of my years in scouting. I always knew that I could survive in the wild, which was of great benefit in my military life during events like survival training.

Sports played a significant part of life for every boy at Tabor. In the first place, it was an all hands requirement to play softball after dinner if weather conditions permitted. Sister Viola, a diminutive taskmaster in charge of the boys' house, was the pitcher for both sides. She was a sports aficionado from Ohio and a big Buckeye's fan during football season. Constant practice honed athletic skills that would pay off in later years as Tabor kids excelled in high school sports programs.

Jake Highton was in the vanguard. He started as end on the football team. He was also a high jumper and middle distance runner on the track team. If there was a common bond among us, it was an obsession with sports. We collected baseball cards, knew all the rules of the game cold, memorized batting averages of major league players and all dreamed of eventually earning a living playing big league baseball. It was the equivalent of attending one of Nick Bollettieri's tennis camps in Florida. You either mastered the skills or were humiliated in the process of failing.

National Farm School was a two year agricultural college about two and one-half miles from Tabor. It produced exciting, hard nosed, single wing football teams. Every Saturday we would make the trek by the 'back road' to watch Farm School humiliate the opposing team. We also made use of their gym to practice basketball during the winter months when snow prevented us from using the outdoor court in back of the boys' house. We thought nothing of walking the five mile round trip. The really hard task was carrying a leather basketball for three miles and not bouncing it on the muddy road enroute to the indoor courts. My Dad was a staunch supporter of any of our athletic endeavors. He kept us supplied with basketballs, footballs and baseball equipment.

Incidentally, he never failed to visit us on Sunday afternoons, riding the bus from Philadelphia. It was a stabilizing influence on my life during those days when cosmic forces seemed to be in control of my fate. It was quite sad to observe about 50 percent of the kids who looked longingly on those lucky enough to have parents visit on the weekends.

If present day child psychologists observed some of the discipline techniques used, they would be aghast. Lynford 'Lympy' Disque, an incorrigible seven-year-old, was actually given coal in his Christmas stocking and nothing else. Among other deeds, Lympy had captured a chicken from the coop behind the boys' house and had buried it alive.

I'm not sure the punishment fit the crime, but the sisters were quite pragmatic about discipline. They would eventually find some means of convincing you to follow the rules. There was relatively little sympathy and a minimum of love given to anyone since that was considered impractical with five or six permanent staff to serve eighty or so children.

In retrospect, two things that were missing from Tabor Home life were a feeling of being loved, and strong role models to give assistance in life counseling. I never developed intellectual curiosity as a child. Education and training were barriers that had to be hurdled. I studied to get good grades, not to absorb facts or understand the philosophy of life. Everyone was lonely. It was part of growing up. You faced the day and put problems like loneliness on the back burner.

In all fairness, it was a nearly impossible task to raise all children successfully. A study by an evaluation team would probably award the Tabor staff fairly high marks.

CHAPTER 3

Doylestown, Pennsylvania

To enjoy the flavor of life, take big bites. Moderation is for monks.

DOYLESTOWN HIGH SCHOOL (DHS) was built in 1889 at a cost of $28,239. Two additions were added in 1912 and 1925. Located in the middle of town, it had been an impressive red granite and brick structure. But in 1947, when I started as a freshman, it was old and in need of replacement. The gym, with its 15-foot ceiling, had not been used for interscholastic basketball games since the early 1930s. The athletic fields were on the west side of town, about a mile from the school. The basketball team practiced and played its games in the town Armory on Shewell Avenue. DHS was in the Bucks and Montgomery County (Bux-Mont) League along with the other towns of Lansdale (Thanksgiving rival), Ambler, Quakertown, Sell-Perk, Hatboro, Souderton, Upper Moreland, and Springfield.

Adjusting to change was never my forte and freshman year in high school was no exception. Coming from Edison Elementary to the big city was a difficult transition for me and the big fish in the small pond gave a minnow-like performance. Not only did the athletic, bright Tabor kid fail to win any varsity letters for his first two years, he also flunked algebra and almost failed Latin. Not a very auspicious start for one who was convinced he couldn't fail in life.

Doylestown itself was a white collar, Republican town of about

5,000 inhabitants who grew up believing in the superiority of their hometown. Only a few black families lived in town and they were prohibited from swimming in the municipal pool. We all accepted that rule and didn't think much about the injustice of it all.

Doylestown had its share of celebrities, not the least of whom was James Michener, who lived there in the teens and twenties. He won the Pulitzer Prize for the musical *South Pacific* in 1950 and had published numerous best-selling novels prior to that award. Michener was the class president of his 1925 DHS high school class and was editor of *The Torch*, the class yearbook. Tabor kids identified with him because we had heard that he was raised in the 'poor house,' about two miles south of Tabor Home on Route 611. Of course, that term would never be used in our 'politically correct' society today but in the 1940s direct speaking people with little sensitivity were common-place. He lived on the north side of Doylestown with his family from 1907 until 1921.

A second well known inhabitant was Oscar Hammerstein, the Broadway lyricist. He lived on the west side of town adjacent to a boyhood friend of mine, Pete Gryson. I played basketball on his inside court on several occasions. I never actually saw Mr. Hammerstein in person but that did not prevent me from bragging that he "lived in my hometown."

Margaret Mead, the famed anthropologist and author, was another alumna of the town. But, since few Tabor kids knew what anthropology was, her name never came up in discussions.

Doylestown was involved in colonial history. The actual founder of the town is unknown, but William Doyle owned a tavern for 30 years on the main street before selling it in 1776 and moving to Hancock, New York. The town was a strategic location for the rebelling colonists to keep an eye on the British in Philadelphia (30 miles to the south) and for getting supplies to General Washington at Valley Forge (20 miles to the south west). In 1778 the Continental Army marched through Doylestown on its way to intercept the British at Monmouth, New Jersey in their retreat from Philadelphia to New

York. Severe weather forced Washington's troops to spend the night in town. Washington actually did sleep in Doylestown though he brought his own tent.

The Pennsylvania General Assembly agreed to move the courthouse from Newtown, located near Philadelphia, to Doylestown, making it the county seat of Bucks County in 1810. It was incorporated as a borough in April 1838 with a population of 900. The introduction of daily train service to Philadelphia 18 years later literally put Doylestown on the map and it increased in population and importance over the next 100 years.

Of my four years in high school, the first period lasted three years and consisted of average to below-average performance. It is a scenario that is not unlike a great many children trying to find themselves in a strange environment and muddling their way through school without defined goals. It is not that I didn't try to excel. A competitive spirit has always been part of my makeup. But, after the successes in elementary school, (class president, successful athlete, graduating near the top of the class) it seemed logical that good fortune would follow me to the next scholastic level. In fact I struggled in Latin and actually failed Algebra I. This from the kid who won the award in eighth grade for the highest average in arithmetic. I almost felt obliged to give back the $2.50. In my defense, the only reason I flunked algebra was because I wasn't changing the sign when subtracting. The following year I aced the course with straight A's and was exempted from taking the final exam.

But during those first three years of high school, there were some successes. I was selected as homeroom representative one year, kicked for the junior varsity (JV) football team, started for the JV basketball team as a junior and managed to earn a varsity 'D' in baseball. I had achieved the pinnacle of success with the opportunity to play in Shibe Park in Philadelphia (major league baseball stadium) for the Eastern Pennsylvania championship in 1949 as part of the 15-year and under American Legion Midget League. We were tied in the last inning when our center fielder, Harry Beer, tried to pick off the opposing runner on second base. Our pitcher threw the ball over Harry's outstretched glove to the center field wall, scoring all three base runners. The upsetting part of that story was that I had just told Harry (as team captain playing left field) not to try such a risky play. My success in the first several years in high school was so limited and I was such an unknown by my classmates that when I was nominated by a friend to run for junior class president, the class secretary wrote my name on the board as Orville Right.

Even the baseball letter that I was awarded was given under curious circumstances. For most of the year I sat on the bench and acted as a bench jockey (i.e. shouted out insults to opposing players to rattle them). I was quite adept at that skill and as soon as it was discovered that a player had 'rabbit ears' (inability to function when verbally criticized), we were unmerciful. With the season coming to a close, the coach decided to play me in a few games as a reward for showing up all season. Much to his surprise, I went on a hitting streak and exhibited base running skills that surprised him. Though I was short of the required number of innings necessary to win a letter, the coach waived the requirement in my case and presented me the coveted 'D.' I sense it was a guilt assuaging exercise on his part for not giving me an opportunity to play all season. I accepted it graciously and wore the letter with great pride.

The second phase of the Doylestown years was my final year in high school. It was a critical 12 month period since a decision on college and career had to be made. The year started out in football camp. I was asked to try out because of my kicking ability as a member of the junior varsity team the year before. Since everyone had to learn a position, I selected halfback and, much to my surprise, I finished camp as the second team right halfback.

After football camp I wrote a humorous story for the high school paper. It was forwarded to the Pennsylvania School Press Association where it won first prize. Here are some excerpts: The field is about three fourths of a mile around. Before and after practice, three times a day, we had to run merrily around the field three times. One day the coach got mad at us just because we were playing games like 'stab the waiter' and he made us run 10 laps around the field. After the completion, he said to us, "You know you're not in shape and a really dedicated football player will take five more laps. Everyone who wants a rest take two steps forward." Everyone on the whole squad stepped forward except our little first year place kicker. The coach put his arm around him and told him how proud he was of him since he was the only player to volunteer to run the extra five laps. "Five more laps" cried the freshman, "I'm too tired to take two steps forward."

Although it was anything but sophisticated humor, it did give me some encouragement in writing and led to eventually performing stand up routines that I blatantly stole from every available source.

Our first game was a non league game against Bensalem, a team we were expected to crush. Several days before the game, Lenny Dauber and Dick Duerr, our starting halfbacks, were caught skipping school and were suspended from all athletics for three weeks. It is an ill wind that blows no one some good. I started the game as both right halfback on offense and safety on defense. Midway through the game, the opposing quarterback completed a pass over the head of the left corner and I was the last remaining hurdle for the touchdown-bound receiver. As he approached, he seemed to hand me the football so I snatched it from his grip and proceeded in the opposite direction with the pigskin. I was finally tackled on the 50 yard line although most of the players and none of the crowd could fathom why I was running north when I should have been preventing their right end, heading south, from scoring. It was quite an unexpected performance from an athlete who had not played a single quarter of high school football before his starting assignment as a two-way player. By the time Duerr was eligible to participate in varsity football again, he had lost his starting role permanently. I started every game, scored two touchdowns and performed well. One of my two touchdowns was a flat-pass thrown by Don Fritz that went for 60 yards, the team's longest run of the season. As it turned out, Don didn't get any credit for it as the reporter misidentified the passer as Harry Beer. In an ironic twist, although I was originally selected to be on the team as a kicker, I sprained my right knee in the preseason and was barely used in that position for the entire year with the exception of a few extra points.

About half way through the football season, the seniors voted for class officers. Our class president the previous year was Virginia James, and she had moved away in 1950, so the election was wide open. It probably helped that I was a varsity football player and a reasonably good public speaker. I wasn't too surprised that the class elected me president. But one of the teachers was overheard to say: "God help us. They've elected a FOOTBALL player to lead the class."

Shortly after losing our final football game to Lansdale on Thanksgiving, basketball season began. Unlike our mediocre football team, Doylestown always fielded basketball teams that were strong contenders in the Bux-Mont league. In 1950, we had four returning starters with a potential all-league center in Jim Radcliff. I started the season at left forward. We won the first few games and the three high scorers were Radcliff, Jack Biester, (the other forward), and me. About the eighth game, disaster struck. Jim broke his right wrist in an awkward fall. The coach decided to move me (at 6 feet one and one-half inches tall) into the center position and fill the forward slot off the bench. Since most of our set plays were designed to use Radcliff's talents, I was given the opportunity to shoot a lot of baskets and score a lot of points. The apex of the season for me was the last home game against Ambler. Here is the quote from Russ Thomas, the sports reporter for the *Doylestown Intelligencer*. "Coach Bob Finn's Doylestown High basketeers lowered the curtain on the home basketball season last night on the Armory floor by defeating Ambler, 61 to 44, to remain in a third place deadlock with Lansdale High (10-5), and one game remaining on the schedule, at Souderton, next Friday night. Two things were outstanding about last night's Bux-Mont games. Hatboro High defeated the rivals from Upper Moreland, by a score of 54 to 42, as predicted by this writer some time ago, and that victory may mean that the Hatters will share the title with Upper Moreland, if Lansdale can defeat the Willow Grove quintet on Friday and Hatboro wins at the same time. The other outstanding highlight of last night's games was the performance tuned in by Orville Wright, Doylestown High senior, playing his last game on the Armory court for DHS. Wright accounted for 31 points, a new Bux-Mont scoring record for the 1950-51 season. The ace center shot nine field goals and converted 13 out of 19 from the charity marker."

The following Friday, we defeated Souderton 59 to 42 and I scored 23 points, which broke another league record for the most points in consecutive games. The local radio station selected me Athlete of the Week and invited me as a talk-show guest on his weekly radio show. The all league selections had just been published and I was selected to the first team. The sportscaster asked me to comment on the fact that Upper Moreland, who had won the conference title, had only one player selected on the first two teams. I responded that it was quite obvious. Upper Moreland had the best defense in the league and won the championship by holding its opponents to low scores. No one recognizes that stellar defenses win basketball games and consequently all players on the first and second all conference teams were selected for their high scoring averages. The host seemed quite impressed that a high school 'jock' could logically respond to an apparently puzzling selection process. He changed the format of the program to allow more time to discuss sports with me.

Although our DHS basketball team made the state playoffs, we lost in the first round to Radnor, a bigger and more talented team. The All Bux-Mont league teams were published and I was selected to the first team. Jack Biester made the second team and both Ted Twining and Tom Redfield made honorable mention. To cap off the season, team members voted for team captain. With Ted Twining the captain his junior year, I realized the vote was going to be very close and I voted for Jack Biester, knowing he had no chance to win. I was elected by a single vote. Such is politics.

During the winter sports season, I became popular enough to be pursued by girls in the class. I had not dated up until senior year for several reasons. First and foremost, I hadn't the wherewithal to ask a girl out. With neither a car nor a surplus of cash, my options were limited. Secondly, the idea of offering support and love to someone else was quite beyond my comprehension. It was not that I was selfish. I was just beginning to figure out what life was all about myself. Sharing that ignorance did not rank high on my list of things to do.

After dating one of the identical Smith twins in the class (I never could sort out who was who) for several weeks, Mary Miller, one of the most popular girls in the class asked me to a Sadie Hawkins Day dance. I was thrilled that she would choose me to be the target of her interest. She was picked homecoming queen later in the year and we attended the prom as honored guests. What a heady environment for a virtual nobody just a year earlier. Life was good!

With a lock on three letters (remember I was a returning baseball letterman), I decided to attempt a fourth by pole vaulting for the track team and perhaps running the quarter mile. If you sense just a touch of arrogance on my part, how could it be helped? I was getting non-requested assistance from somewhere. How else could one explain the events that allowed me to win a starting berth in football and create a situation on the basketball team that resulted in overwhelming plaudits and recognition? But I was about to learn a lesson about sporting successes. As in the stock market, there are peaks and valleys in athletic endeavors. Yesterday's heroes are today's also-rans. Breaking my wrist while pole-vaulting in practice quickly ended my quest for four letters in a single year. The school immediately changed policies and banned all baseball players from participating in track.

As this unusual year came to a close, there were additional surprises. The senior class voted me both the most popular boy (along with Henry Klein) and the best male athlete. Upon reflection, it should have been obvious that Tom Redfield was the more accomplished athlete and deserved the honor. Incidentally, Tom married Marty Hoover, selected best female athlete, and settled in California raising quite a successful family. I hosted Marty and her daughter, Brenda, to an evening meal on board the USS New Orleans 20 years later in Long Beach, California. Because the vote was taken right after basketball season, emotional rather than objective reasoning was probably responsible for the miscarriage of justice. Years later, when scanning my high school year book and discovering that the class had selected me most popular, my teenaged stepdaughter, Jenelle, asked the question, "What kind of weird high school class did you have, anyway?"

The usual end of school activities such as senior class banquet and commencement pushed me into the spotlight since I was class president and acted as toastmaster or introduced the graduation speaker. There seemed to be no limit on my aspirations as long as it didn't require a lot of money. I received a nice congratulatory letter from a member who was on the Tabor Home Board of Directors along with a check for $100 ($960.00 if given today). Here are a few lines from his letter: "You have no idea what a satisfaction people who are connected with Tabor Home feel when we realize the splendid job you did for yourself and your Alma Mater. The Home also has been helped by your record, since it can be no better than the youngsters it produces. I hope that you are determined to carry on your educational program and training. My hat's off to you, lad. Keep your target high and carry on."

I managed to graduate with honors but there were six others out of 119 in the class who actually attained highest honors. My basic intelligence quotient (IQ) was high enough to compete but I regret that I never possessed sufficient intellectual curiosity. I studied to pass tests, not to gain knowledge. Formal education would have been so much simpler had I just possessed that one characteristic.

My social life took a hiatus between high school graduation and prep school when the 'love of my life' lost interest. I learned from another friend that Mary's mother didn't think it was such a good idea to get serious with someone with such a limited future. I might have spent more time lamenting my fate if my plate had not been so full.

In addition to working for the Doylestown Borough as a common laborer, I also played American Legion summer baseball. I was the only Doylestown player selected for the All Star game that attracted a number of big league scouts. I went 0 for 2 and had my chance to impress the big boys in the fifth inning. Playing first base, I had concocted a clever pickoff play with my catcher before the game. If there were men on first and second, or if the bases were loaded, I would touch the bill of my cap. The catcher would acknowledge the plan to throw behind the runner leading off first base by touching his mask. With the bases loaded and the opposing team's power hitter at the plate, I touched my cap and received the catcher's sign that the next pitch would be the pickoff throw to first base. Unfortunately, the batter hit the pitch for a triple and cleared the bases. So much for impressing the scouts.

CHAPTER 4

Preparatory School

Only a mediocre person is always at his best.

AS COLLEGE YEARS approached, it was obvious that some sort of tuition free school would be required. Unlike educational opportunities for higher education now, only about 10 percent of high school graduates matriculated to institutions of higher learning. Consequently, aid, loans, and grants were unusual. An obvious choice was the Military Academy at West Point. Plebe year couldn't be any harder than Tabor Home indoctrination and the government would actually pay you to get an education. With those dubious ground rules established, the plan was hatched. The scheme underwent a modification almost immediately when one of Dad's customers at the Custom Shop at Wanamaker's department store turned out to be Rip Miller (one of the seven blocks of granite who blocked for the Four Horsemen of Notre Dame in 1924). Miller was the assistant athletic director at the Naval Academy and he expressed an interest in recruiting any promising athlete.

Navy had powerhouse football teams in the 1940s and 1950s before the days of million dollar contracts in the National Football League. They used four or five prep schools to prepare potential athletes for the academic rigors of the Academy. I was invited down to Annapolis by Rip Miller to see the grounds and convince me to apply for entrance. You can imagine that it did not take much of an effort to sell me on the advantages of life at the Naval Academy. I was especially impressed when he took me out to lunch at a yacht club and simply signed for the lunch. Quite awesome.

A strategy was conceived to apply for a scholarship to Wyoming Seminary near Wilkes-Barre, Pa., while requesting an appointment from my local congressman. In addition, it was recommended that I join the Naval Reserve so I could take a competitive examination for one of 75 slots it was allotted. The die was cast.

The summer of 1951 was spent working for the Borough of Doylestown repairing roads and laying sewer pipes. The pay was $1.05 an hour and we worked 44 hours a week. Since this was my first paying job, I decided to buy a car with my summer earnings. Never mind about car insurance, car repair bills or gas. With the $300 that I accumulated, I purchased a 1939 Oldsmobile costing $300.

I volunteered to drive Jake Highton back to Penn State in August in my newly acquired black Olds. Half way to State College, Pa., a front right wheel bearing failed and we spent the rest of the day towing the car to a local mechanic and hitchhiking with all of Jake's worldly goods to his fraternity. After a good night's sleep, I got back on the road and thumbed a ride back to Tabor to formulate a plan to recover my car.

After listening to my tale of woe, one of the young deaconesses, Sister Harriet Scott, loaned me $50 to retrieve my beloved automobile. Actually, my love was starting to fade by now. The desire for wheels, which burned so intensely all summer, was being tempered by the realization that my new acquisition was costly, frustrating and did not produce the gratification that I had imagined. Owning the 'freedom machine' came with some subtle caveats. It could only be driven weekends at prep school and then only with someone who possessed gas money. Buying a car as a cash poor student has to rank high on the list of emotional decisions I regret making.

After the Pennsylvania mechanic called the school and told them my car was repaired and ready for pickup, the principal's curiosity was aroused as to who actually owned the vehicle since student automobiles were prohibited at Wyoming Seminary. When I responded that it was my father's, he seemed relieved. Several weeks later, I sold my magnificent chariot for a paltry $50. I still owe Sister Harriett the $50 I borrowed from her to get it out of hock. If any reader knows her location and contacts me, I will willingly repay my one outstanding debt with interest. I catalogue this memorable event under 'Unmitigated Disasters.' The car file is closed.

Wyoming Seminary was founded in 1844 by the Methodist church to ensure that young Protestant boys and girls received a sound education with a religious flavor. Only a few academies and seminaries, supported by religious denominations or neighborhoods, provided education beyond grade school. From an initial class size of 31, housed in one building, the school expanded to over 500 college-bound students in the upper school, which now sported over 12 modern educational buildings in the complex. Over the years, the school was able to maintain both athletic and scholastic excellence by establishing firm standards and high expectations for its students.

I reported into Carpenter Hall (boys' dorm) on the first day of school and met my roommate, Eugene Alderman from Endicott, N.Y. He and several other Union-Endicott (UE) High School attendees decided to prep at Wyoming Seminary before enrolling in a university. His father owned the largest Studebaker dealership in the Southern Tier of New York and he played both football and basketball. We got along very well and have maintained a friendship for 50 years. I spent one Easter vacation at his house in Endicott and had a great time. Little did I know that my first civilian job would take me to the Southern Tier and I would actually live there considerably longer than Gene. He joined IBM and spent most of his working career in Atlanta. The school yearbook described him as having dark hair, handsome, and easy to get along with. It also commented on his sports interest, particularly football. The final statement was that, 'Gene was Wright's roommate and still remained sane.'

Although I knew next to nothing about Wyoming Seminary when I reported there in September 1951, I was fairly confident of success. I not only graduated from a college preparatory course at Doylestown High School but was also an athlete that Navy was interested in. How hard could a prep school be?

What I didn't know was how talented the athletes were who were being sent to Sem to prepare for the big time. We had a contingent of Navy-bound students that numbered about 20. Twelve or 13 were football players and on the first day I wandered over to the practice field with the thought in the back of my mind to try out. Mind you, I had been a below average halfback in a high school that won about one half its games in a fairly weak league. After a cursory look at the size, speed and obvious skill level of the players, I decided to concentrate on basketball and baseball. Five of those 13 started for the Navy varsity football team that beat Ole Miss in the Sugar Bowl. George Welsh from Coaldale, Pa. was the quarterback who would lead Navy to three successful seasons and be selected an honorable mention all-American. John Hopkins from Brooklyn, N.Y., played end and would captain the 1956 Navy team. Jim Royer, from the Philadelphia suburbs, played right tackle and would be a two year starter for USNA. Dick Guest played halfback and turned into one of Navy's superb punters. Ron Beagle from Covington, Ky., was the most talented pass catcher I have ever seen. He would be a consensus all-American selection his final year at Navy. With that crew, the Blue Knights of Wyoming Seminary lost just two games (Navy and Bullis Prep) with wins over Columbia Prep, Cornell Frosh, Valley Forge, Perkiomen, and Carteret.

Christmas break that year was spent at Tabor Home where they treated me like a returning hero. Tabor kids, Will and Don Fritz, were juniors at Central Bucks High (the new name of Doylestown High) and were establishing themselves as bona fide superstars in football, basketball and baseball. Tabor kids were feeling proud to be from the Home and outsiders were expressing some envy of the girls who got to live with all the popular athletes. That was quite a turn about in just a few years.

January brought the start of basketball season and I was confident of having a good season. We had an all-state forward from Ohio (John Zban) and an honorable mention all-state point guard from Pittsburgh (Tommy Loughran). The addition of 6-foot 7-inch Ed Chesney at center would ensure that we got our share of rebounds. With a 13-game schedule against the likes of college freshmen and JV teams, we knew we wouldn't have too many easy contests.

We won five of our first seven games and I ended up leading the team in scoring with an 18-point average. We then lost three in a row against the freshmen teams at Lafayette and Cornell as well as the JV team at Lehigh. We managed to win two of the last three games and completed the season with a seven-win, six-loss record. One of the losses I blame on the coach who pulled the first team with the score 25-11 in the first period and allowed Lehigh to close within four points at half time. By the time we had recovered our momentum, two of our starters had fouled out and despite outscoring them in the final period, we lost by 12 points. The second time we played them on our home court, they beat us by two points in overtime. The lesson here is to roll up the score when your team is hot.

We traveled to our away games via the coaches' automobiles. En route to Bucknell University for our first game, there were five players packed into a mid-size sedan as we drove along a three-lane highway. The middle lane was designed for passing for both north and south traffic. I was sitting on the driver's side in the back seat when I saw a car accelerate past us just as a car coming in the opposite direction also pulled out to pass. The head-on collision occurred just yards ahead of us, and the flying debris exiting both cars damaged the left side of the car directly in front of us. We stopped to assist the injured but other good Samaritans were already on the scene. The piercing sound of crunching, disintegrating metal left a lasting impression on me. Several years later Pennsylvania outlawed all three-lane highways due to the high fatality rate on these 'killer' roads.

Two weeks later the team was returning from Allentown in January when we encountered a snowstorm. Despite our creep speed, the car lost traction coming down a slight incline and started sliding side-ways. As we skidded off the highway the auto turned upside down, as though we were in slow motion. As the sedan started the turnover, I recall saying "Here we go." The memory that remained, after asking if everyone was uninjured, was rolling the back window up to crawl out of the turtle-like car.

Periodically, the class would combine a dance with a variety or talent show, which they called a Blue and White (school colors). Here is an article in the school newspaper following one such event: *Blue and White* – Orville Wright. "Our Blue and White program was a success two Saturday nights ago with Orville Wright giving a merry half hour of pure wit. Paul Chaddock's rendition of a man's life from a little boy giving his first recital to an older man playing his last, plus narration by Orville, kept us guffawing. But nothing could surpass Claude Bunion, Foot Detective. (The actual sketch was Sam Club, Foot Detective but perhaps the reporter wanted to soften the title.) All together, it was an evening much enjoyed with the right records being played, jitterbugging and Paul Chaddock on the piano. Tune in next week to hear what happened to...Claude Bunion, Foot Detective."

During basketball season I also met my second girlfriend, a junior at the school named Dottie Funke. She played field hockey, was an attractive blond and had a younger sister in the lower school that thought I was a white knight that had simply misplaced my horse. Her father was a surgeon and they lived about 10 miles from the school. I still lacked the savoir-faire to make the relationship very meaningful but it was nice to have a pretty girl interested in you. Dottie married successfully after completing two years at Goucher College and we still correspond 65 years later.

Midway through the school year I read some disconcerting news about the congressman Albert Vaughn from the eighth District (Doylestown) of Pennsylvania. He suffered a heart attack and died without actually nominating me for the appointment to the Naval Academy. He had released the test results and announced that I had attained the highest score but the nomination was to come later. This was a real

35

dilemma for someone who had a very limited backup plan, which consisted of joining the Naval Reserve Unit in Kingston, PA, and competing for one of the 75 slots available to reserve enlisted men. Fortunately, the new congressman, Karl King, honored the test results given by his predecessor and announced my appointment in January 1952.

Speaking of competing for the hallowed appointments, the 16 student-athletes at Sem seemed to have a 'cooperate and graduate' mentality, which transferred to the competitive exams for entrance to the USNA. On the day of the Naval Reserve test, one of the football players positioned himself between two of the smartest candidates, Eb Eaton and Bob Harris. Both Eb and Bob scored high but the one who landed on the top of the heap was the halfback who compared both answers and decided which was better. It did require some amount of skill to discriminate between two good answers but he couldn't have felt real pride when the test results were announced.

Baseball season arrived in April and first year Coach Bob Weaver had great credibility since he had pitched in the minor leagues (affiliated with the Philadelphia Athletics) for a number of years until injuries finished his career. We had a successful eight-game season and won most of our games. I believe I hit in every game and played center field. I don't recall my batting average but it was over 300.

From an academic standpoint, Wyoming Seminary set an expectation of excellence clearly above Doylestown High since 98 percent of the student body planned to pursue continuing education. I can't say I loved the academic portion of prep school since I viewed attaining acceptable grades as a means to accomplish my goal of preparing myself to cope with the complex maze of the Naval Academy. There were a number of teachers that come to mind while reminiscing about my post-high school education.

- Miss Helen Brown seemed to teach more than English. She took it personally if you didn't get involved in her classes. Every student thought she cared about him or her. That is truly a gift.

- Professor Hughes - Although out of touch with the world of students, there was no doubt he had their best interests at heart.
- Dean Adams was the quintessential administrator. He was not only an excellent math teacher but also really liked solving students' problems.
- Professors Bob Weaver and Ben Kennedy were excellent coaches and history teachers.
- Robert Stultz would make science interesting and meaningful.

I graduated from Sem with fond memories. My classmates voted me both the most popular and the most humorous guy in the class of 1952. Stepdaughter Jenelle would be convinced that both senior classes got it all wrong.

The short summer consisted of playing American Legion baseball for Doylestown again. A really good season for me and I was, once again, selected (along with Don Fritz) for the All Star game in July. Out of forty players, the scouts selected six (including me) to represent Eastern Pennsylvania. I was on the roster as number 16 and playing first base. But in reality I was being sworn in at the Naval Academy in Annapolis as the game was being played in Shibe Park, Philadelphia. Years later, my stepson, Jeffrey, chastised me for passing up my "once in a lifetime" opportunity to play in the big leagues. To me, it was a no-brainer.

CHAPTER 5

Midshipman Days

I drive way too fast to worry about my cholesterol level.

THERE IS NO doubt that the U.S. Naval Academy, located on the Severn River in historic Annapolis, capital of Maryland, is a glamorous place, as long as you're not a midshipman. It was designed to fill parents' hearts with pride upon seeing their sons and daughters standing at attention in faultless ranks at noon formation in front of the venerable Bancroft Hall. Emotions can hardly be contained as the brigade, adorned in a sea of blue, khaki or white, smartly marches off to the strains of a patriotic John Philip Sousa march.

From a midshipman's viewpoint, a zoo analogy may be apropos. As pleasant as a zoo is to the visitors, it is not great fun for the animals that have starring roles in the drama. They are fed and housed but their freedom is severely limited and there is a price to pay if they don't follow the script. ('Absolutely no eating of visitors, particularly the very small ones. Violators of this rule will be dealt with severely.')

The basic issue with the Naval Academy is that the system requires midshipmen to accomplish a finite number of tasks in a set number of hours. However, the hours available to a midshipman are less than the set number. Hence, a time management problem exists with each student graded on his priorities. Virtually no one conquers the system. You are graded by how badly you fail. The upper classes are charged with discouraging the plebes (1st year students) through humiliation and harassment so they will resign. This does not even address the work required to pass a challenging engineering curriculum.

The Naval Academy is a government operated school whose mission is to educate and train young men and women to become officers in the United States Navy and Marine Corps. Students at the Academy are called midshipmen (with the emphasis on the mid) and successful completion of the four year course results in both a commission in a military service plus a Bachelor of Science (B.S.) degree.

In 1952, when I entered, the reality of female midshipmen was two and one-half decades in the future and there was a single, lock-step academic program for every student with the only exception being a choice of a foreign language. It was a basic scientific curriculum with emphasis on marine (maritime) engineering, mathematics, science and professional subjects such as navigation, gunnery, seamanship, and leadership. The summers were spent learning the practical side of being a naval officer by cruising on ships, visiting naval air stations and getting flights in aircraft as well as participating in amphibious exercises. From this exposure to various aspects of naval warfare, you would be in a better position to select your choice of service or warfare specialty. Since this was before the advent of the Air Force Academy in Colorado, 25 percent of the graduating class could select the U.S. Air Force.

Entrance to the Academy is primarily by congressional appointment although 85 slots per class were set aside for enlisted men in the regular and reserve Navy. In addition, there were openings for children of deceased and disabled veterans. A third category was Presidential appointees who, as sons of active duty members, scored high on the entrance exam. About 40 members in our class gained entrance through this channel. Most candidates applied through their congressman or senator, who generally gave a competitive exam to determine who would be awarded the appointment. There was no requirement on the part of the congressman to open the appointment to competition. He or she could simply award it to their nephew or to a friend or donor's child. For those who scored high on the exam but were not given the appointment, the Academy could grant them entrance as "qualified alternates" to fill out the class. My roommate at the Academy, Harold Dolenga, gained entrance through that route when his congressman from Detroit told him he was obliged to give his primary appointment to a friend's son, but he (the congressman) was confident that the appointee would fail the entrance exam. He was correct.

Midshipmen were provided tuition, room and board, and medical and dental care. In addition, they were paid a salary. The year I entered, a midshipman paid for his books, uniforms, equipment, and services out of a monthly salary of $111, which left him in debt for about three years. Repayment was required if the student submitted his resignation prior to graduation. In his first year, a plebe was given a monthly stipend of $3 in cash to pay for movies or a soft drink in town. Midshipmen accepted a *de facto* vow of poverty.

The history of the Academy is revealing with some of its traditions. Before 1845, midshipmen were trained and educated exclusively on frigates at sea under the tutelage of a schoolmaster. In 1842, Midshipman Spencer was hanged on board the Navy school ship *Somers* for planning a mutiny. Normally, an event like this would not have created much of a stir in the country since commanding officers at sea had capital punishment authority. In this case, however, the hanged midshipman was the son of the Secretary of War. George Bancroft, Secretary of the Navy, made an immediate decision to replace all Navy school ships with a naval school to be located at Fort Severn. It was a two year program followed by three years at sea, and then a final year at school aboard the practice frigate before taking the lieutenant's exam. The course of study was identical to that of the Military Academy at West Point, which had been functioning since 1802. Several years later the course of instruction was changed from six to four years and the name was officially designated U.S. Naval Academy (USNA). The Academy was the sole source of naval officers until 1917.

In the early 1920's a number of reforms was instituted. Midshipmen were granted Christmas and Easter leave. They were also allowed to smoke, play cards and subscribe to a newspaper for the first time. It was not until 1947 that the first classmen (seniors) were permitted to own cars and, if outside the seven mile radius of the state house, drink alcoholic beverages. For most of its history, the Academy was a very conservative institution and changes in culture did not come easily. They did not have an African-American graduate until 1949.

The Association of American Universities accredited the Academy in 1930 and, nine years later, Congress bestowed the degree of B.S. upon all living graduates retroactively. It took twenty more years to use the College Education Examination Board as criteria for acceptance. There is an age requirement that stipulates you must be 17 years old by July 1 of the year of admission and cannot be older than 21 on the same date. Logically, one would think the older the midshipmen, the more likely they would be to handle the institutionalized stress and one would know if they wanted to be a career naval officer. Statistics indicate otherwise, with older midshipmen having a higher dropout rate than their younger counterparts. The same was true of student pilots with the younger men having a higher success rate of completion. The average class, prior to 1970, would lose about one-third of its students in the four year curriculum, with 90 percent of that number happening within the first 12 months. My class (1956) ended up with an attrition rate that exceeded one-third.

Midshipmen rooms were certainly livable with two, three, or four students to a room with three being the most common. There was a shower as well as a bathroom sink in the room and a desk, chair, and locker for each midshipman. One person was responsible for the cleanliness of the room and that responsibility rotated weekly. Any officer inspecting a room simply had to look at the occupant's nametag above the door to identify which of the two or three members would be put on report for not having a shipshape room.

When I reported for duty at the Academy in July 1952, a naval career was the farthest thing from my mind. I knocked on the

Superintendent of Midshipmen's door in accordance with my orders and was informed midshipmen did not report to the admiral himself. It probably wouldn't have gone down well to let Rear Admiral Harry Hill (Hill was relived by Vadm. Turner Joy on August 4th) know that my purpose in reporting was to play basketball and baseball in exchange for a free education.

The announced purpose of plebe summer was to bridge the gap between civilian life and midshipman life. The brigade officers are charged with assisting in this transition. By assist they mean instill discipline, develop leadership qualities and introduce midshipmen to nautical and military aspects of a career in the naval service. Brigade officers, by and large, are newly graduated ensigns and second lieutenants on temporary additional duty awaiting an assignment to such things as flight training. The six or seven weeks of plebe summer is a whirlwind of learning the nautical language, increasing your physical fitness, getting your uniforms stenciled and marked, studying Reef Points (a small manual that delineates a lot of useful as well as superfluous information), finding out what plebe year was all about, and realizing first year midshipmen had no idea what Academy life was like, even after visiting the place several times.

To celebrate the end of plebe summer, we were given a party across the Severn River and I emceed a plebe talent show. My opening remarks were, "To think I gave up three years of medical school for this." Four years later a classmate approached me and said: "Didn't you go to medical school before the Academy?" I replied: "Of course not. Whatever made you think that?" It wasn't until much later that I remembered that line during plebe summer.

One other event occurring that summer stood out in my memory. I had requested to study Russian since I had only taken Latin in high school. I was sure that if I signed up for Russian it would be a level playing field with no one having an advantage of studying Russian in high school. With a language proficiency that was laughable, I quickly discovered the fallacy in my logic of choosing the most difficult language the Academy offered. I submitted a written request to switch to the much easier Portuguese language, but I failed to spell Portuguese properly and the request was rejected with a notation to resubmit with proper spelling. I simply balled up the rejected request and threw it in the trashcan. This rash decision came back to haunt me later in the year.

The plebe baseball team played a full schedule of games under the watchful eye of the varsity coach Max Bishop, former second baseman for the Philadelphia Athletics from 1925 to 1935. His nickname was 'camera eye' because of the large number of times he received base-on-balls during his playing days. Max took a shine to me and occasionally used me as an example when making a point to the team. It also helped that I had a good season both at bat and in centerfield. Plebe summer ended quickly and the upper class showed up on schedule in September.

I was assigned to the 14th Company (out of 24 brigade-wide) on the fourth deck of Bancroft Hall, a humongous student dorm with 33 acres of floor space and nearly five miles of corridors. My two assigned roommates were Hal Dolenga from Detroit and Clyde (Hoppy) Hohenstein, a Navy junior (one whose father is or has been on active duty) who lived various places growing up. On average, one out of every three plebes would fail to graduate. We defied the odds. All three of us graduated and we all retired from the Navy after successful careers; Hal in the Supply Corps, Hoppy as a submariner and me as a helicopter test pilot.

Life as a plebe revolved around academics, athletics and "professional development," which is a nice way of saying learning enough about the Navy and midshipman life to stay out of trouble with upperclassmen. No one could be completely successful as a plebe because the system did not allow it. But keeping a reasonably low profile and feigning humbleness went a long way toward reaching the ultimate goal of attaining total invisibility. You could never, ever take things personally because that would lead to your downfall. The entire brigade was a stage and you were but a bit player. To my knowledge, there was no physical hazing at the Academy, but the mental harassment was virtually non-stop for nine months. It varied from come-arounds, which was an invitation to the room of an upperclassman for special instruction, to singing a cappella the fight song of a college or university that Navy was scheduled to play that week. Special instruction might consist of announcing chow call.

Chow call was a standard format of standing outside the upperclassman's room before each meal and reciting the time until formation (the entire brigade would form in ranks), the uniform required, the published menu, and the identification of the Officers of the Watch as well as the Midshipman Officer of the Watch. This might be announced every five minutes until you had just enough time to make it to formation yourself. The come-around lasted from a single time to a two or three week sentence, depending on the mood of the upperclassman.

On occasion, the fox outwitted the hounds. We had a classmate in the 14th Company named Les Johnson, who was seemingly tone-deaf and sang every song with just a single note. He was a favorite target of many of the upperclassmen who sent him around to all their friends and had Les serenade them. They never found out that Les played the violin and actually had a good singing voice. By playing the fool, he distracted the tormentors and it furnished Les with a free ride (no additional plebe tasks). It was a dangerous game to play, but he pulled it off for much of the year.

Recognizing the drastic change in lifestyles for incoming plebes, the Academy assigned a first-classman (senior) to each plebe, to act as a mentor and quasi-friend. They were often a big help to a beleaguered and confused 18 year old who found himself in the middle of an Alice-in-Wonderland scenario. It also challenged the plebe's problem solving abilities that had served him so well up to then. My first classman was of limited help, and although he seemed sympathetic to my plight, did little in the way of answering professional questions.

In all fairness, perhaps he felt I didn't need much assistance. He had so little impact on my life that I don't even recall his name.

However, many of my classmates have nothing but the highest regard for their 'firsties' and have remained life-long friends.

With every midshipman required to participate in either a varsity or intramural sport each season, I decided to run intramural cross country during the fall season of plebe year. I was defeated only once during the season, but I hated every race, since my concept of sport is that it be fun. Running for the sake of running is decidedly not fun. My strategy was always the same; the course was level for the first 150 yards before a steep upgrade of about 200 yards. I would sprint up the hill even though it was very tiring. Opposing runners often found that being passed so decisively on the hardest part of the course was completely demoralizing to them and they seldom recovered. Despite feeling sick to my stomach following every race, I continued to use the tactic successfully the whole season. The only bright side of that year was that one usually got to 'carry-on' if his company team was victorious in a sporting event. That meant that instead of sitting at attention with your eyes looking straight ahead and speaking only in reply to a question, you are permitted to look around and are excused from harassment during meals. It was one of the reasons plebes root so ardently during the Army football game. A Navy victory automatically means all plebes carry-on until Christmas break. A 7-0 victory over Army in 1952 was the best possible present a plebe could receive. Looking back, it is hard to believe that happiness revolved around some upperclassman giving you a two-finger indication to carry-on.

Christmas leave was a godsend. Instead of constant harassment from upperclassmen, you are suddenly the center of attention in your hometown and looking splendid in your blue uniform. I even double-dated with Jack Biester and his girl friend, Jane Hennessy, who was rooming in New York City with a Rockette from Radio City Music Hall. My blind date was attractive, a good dancer and she also seemed enamored of me. I would like to believe it wasn't the uniform, but I'm afraid that was the overriding factor. I returned to Annapolis with improved morale.

The winter season was basketball and I was optimistic about starting for the plebes even though there were quite a number of outstanding players competing to make the squad. During plebe summer, the varsity squash coach paid me a visit and said he saw me playing baseball and invited me out for squash. I was flattered that the coach would invite me personally since his teams were perennial champions, but I turned him down because it was played during basketball season. He replied that he doubted I could make the plebe squad, but I did make the team although ending up on the second team.

Halfway through the season, disaster struck. I failed the Russian mid-year exam with a 2.3 (58%) and my daily grades were not high enough to allow me to pass the course. Suddenly my rash decision not to resubmit my request to change languages flashed through my head. I was permitted to retake the exam and passed it so I was reinstated immediately. For about a week it looked as if my naval career was over.

There were other midshipmen who were not so fortunate and were dismissed. In fact, out of 1,052 plebes who were sworn in on that warm July day in 1952, only 681 survived to graduate four years later, a dropout rate of 35 percent. To many, the thought of returning home and admitting failure to friends and family was totally overwhelming.

A few souls took a drastic step, committing suicide by jumping off the top floor at Bancroft Hall. This irreversible solution must seem incomprehensible, but to a hometown hero who has known only success and adulation, the humiliation of returning as a failure was intolerable.

Things in general improved in the second half of plebe year. Everyone became familiar with the system and learned to avoid the upperclassmen that tended to make life miserable. Academics took a more prominent place as professional development was given shorter shrift. By spending more time on Russian, I even managed to attain a grade of 3.0 (B-). Spring also had a positive effect on the entire brigade of midshipmen. The first classmen seemed much more concerned about impending career choices and tended to ignore the plebes. We could not have been happier.

As plebe baseball season started, I had some misgivings when I found out that Joe Duff had been assigned as plebe baseball coach. He was brought to the Academy to assist Ben Carnevale with basketball. He knew virtually nothing about baseball, but was available in the spring for coaching duties. The first rule he instituted was that no player was permitted to switch-hit. Every player must choose to bat either left or right-handed with no exception. Since I was the only player that hit from both sides of the plate, I felt this was a slap at me personally. I chose left since there were more right-handed pitchers in the league, but I wasn't thrilled about being prevented from hitting right-handed (my natural stance) against lefties. The team had a winning season and I ended the year with the highest batting average among all the outfielders. I felt quite confident about making the varsity the following year.

Meanwhile in Doylestown, my Brother Will had graduated from high school and was selected as the 'best personality' in his class. He signed up to attend Wyoming Seminary and planned to apply for entrance to the Naval Academy.

June Week (last week of academics) came and Larry Smith fixed me up with a friend of his fiancé. She was a very nice Catholic girl and, as many of my classmates embarked on the cruiser Macon, we promised we'd stay in touch. I never saw or heard from her again. But who can worry about such things when cruising to Brazil and Barbados?

Third class cruise was memorable on several counts. It marked the end of plebe year, which was a milestone in any midshipman's life. The ship crossed the equator en route to South America, turning us into 'shellbacks.' It marked the first time I was out of the continental United States. It also gave fledgling midshipmen their first look at life in the seagoing Navy. Cruisers are huge ships, several football fields in length with about a 40-foot draft (distance below the waterline) and masts that extend 140-foot above the main deck. The main deck is constructed of wood overlaid on steel and the method of keeping the decks ship-shape is via a 'holy stone.' The soft sandstone, first used in the early 19th century for this purpose, is moved back and forth with 4-foot broom handles that fit into a depression on the stone. This is a manual operation with the horsepower generated from enlisted men or third class midshipmen. It was done weekly to ensure the white timbers show their finest grain to inspecting officers or visitors. Other tasks assigned to midshipman were chipping paint, cleaning bilges, (located on the bottom hull of a ship) and standing watches. A cruiser has nine 8-inch guns on its main deck. The '8-inch' is the diameter of the shell that is fired a distance of about 20 miles, which amounts to awesome firepower.

Before we docked in Sao Paulo, the Macon made a stop in Barbados. Several memories survive that visit in 1953. First, the taxi drivers drove like Formula One candidates. I am sure the fatality rate among drivers on the island ranks up there with Portugal (about three times that of the United States). I overheard one midshipman telling the driver he was in a hurry to get back to the ship just so he could see the look of astonishment on all the pedestrians along the way. Also, the midshipmen received an invitation to play a basketball game against the top team on Barbados. A group of us formed a makeshift team and defeated them handily. They were still shooting with two hands similar to U.S. players in the 1930s. After the game, several of their players asked if we had ever played the Globetrotters. We were all quite flattered with that compliment.

Crossing the equator on a Navy ship was fairly unusual in 1953 because not many Navy ships sailed into the southern hemisphere. There was a full-day ritual culminating in a 'dash-to-salvation' by all the uninitiated (pollywogs) on their hands and knees through a long line of 'shellbacks' armed with shillelaghs (paddles). Rank was meaningless and any number of officers nursed bruised bottoms for the next few weeks. I am a little ashamed to admit that I put a soft cover book in my underpants, which softened the blows considerably. If the shellbacks had discovered my secret, I would have reentered the line with a special designation pinned on my back. As they say in Naval Air, 'no guts, no glory.'

In the shower room immediately after the initiation, I had some pangs of remorse when I observed the swollen and discolored backsides of my colleagues. However, this temporary state of contrition could be measured in nanoseconds. There is a certain smug satisfaction in beating the system, but in this case, there was no one with whom to share the story.

Later in the cruise, the midshipmen put on a talent show for the ship's crew. I did a standup routine as detective Sam Club and that type of humor was perfect for the ship's company. Actually, when you are at sea for weeks at a time, it is quite easy to amuse the audience. I discussed a murder case I was working on when I came across this beautiful female suspect. "As I walked into the darkened room, I realized she had no clothes on. From nowhere she drew a gun." That was my type of humor. After the show, one of the enlisted men came up to me and said: "You are one of the funniest comedians I have ever heard. What are you doing in the Navy?" To this day, his remarks rank as one of the most flattering compliments I have ever received.

As the first large foreign country I had ever visited, Brazil was quite impressive. Both Sao Paulo and Rio de Janeiro were modern cities with skyscrapers, modern airports and large numbers of people. Sao Paulo had about five million and Rio numbered about four million. A building boom was underway in both cities and it was not unusual to see thirty story office buildings with no plumbing or electrical wiring because the builder had gone bankrupt and abandoned the contract. I was struck by the beauty of the Brazilian women, especially on the beach at Copacabana. Rio's location on Guanabara Bay with Sugar Loaf Mountain in the background made it the most impressive city I had seen up until that time. Perhaps only Sydney, Australia, can compare with Rio for sheer beauty.

Upon completing this youngster (sophomore) cruise, a 30-day leave was granted and the anticipation of it was probably as enjoyable as the actual vacation. When I arrived at Tabor like a returning hero, everyone was anxious to hear tales of midshipman life as well as travels to the Caribbean and South America. After all, it was not every day a favorite son returned home.

For summer activities, Tabor Home would often hire additional staff consisting of college girls majoring in social work or home economics. One such girl was working in the boys' dorm that summer and it did not take long to get acquainted. Her name was Donna Sulouff and she was attending Mansfield State Teachers College in Mansfield, Pennsylvania. Her major was home economics and she planned to teach in high school. Donna was quite attractive and by the time the summer was over, an initial bonding had taken place. She was two years older and about two decades wiser regarding interpersonal relationships. For the next three years, she was my only girlfriend and it became apparent that we would get married after graduation.

I spent at least part of every holiday at her house in Northumberland, Pennsylvania. I became quite close to her family, which consisted of her father William, her mother Dorothy, her older brother Nelson, her older sister Vernetta, and her younger brother Ernest. The Sulouff family was Pennsylvania Dutch (German extraction) with strong ties to the Lutheran Church. Donna's siblings were quite talented and bright. Nelson graduated from college in three years near the top of his class and became a Navy chaplain. Vernetta chose to marry a local farmer and raise a family but there was never any doubt how smart, organized and innovative she was. Ernest loved airplanes and planned to become an aerospace engineer at Penn State, but he changed his mind after one semester and took a less challenging major.

Youngster (third class) year was a huge improvement with regard to money ($5 monthly instead of $3), love (steady girl friend with a car), and dreams (focus on graduating). Academics became a bit easier and professional courses such as navigation, seamanship, and gunnery were being introduced. I found the naval-related courses quite boring. I did not realize until a few years later that the reason they were boring was that the instructors were not too enthused about teaching those subjects and did not make them come alive. When I got into the fleet, I found those subjects fascinating.

Meanwhile, Will had graduated from Central Bucks and was following my footsteps by enrolling at Wyoming Seminary. He also started for both their basketball and baseball teams. He planed to enter the Naval Academy via the Naval Reserve competitive exam. I never knew what his motivation was to attend the Academy but I suspect it was similar to mine.

I always secretly admired his no sweat attitude in life, but my personality would not permit such an approach. It seemed to work very well for him. He always seemed to attract the most desirable women and his athletic successes were impressive. His way was not as effective in academics, but his motto that any grade points in excess of the minimum were an unnecessary effort, worked for him.

My one big disappointment in third class year was varsity baseball. As the leading plebe outfielder, I knew I was in contention to start for the varsity, especially playing for Max Bishop. I was shocked when the list was posted to find out I had been cut from the team. The following day I asked Max why. "Joe Duff black-balled you and I had to support his decision since he was the plebe coach," Max replied. I can only surmise the reason that Joe blackballed me was because he sensed I knew he was faking his knowledge about baseball and wanted to establish his authority.

As a result of my disappointment, I concentrated on intramural sports consisting of soccer, touch football and basketball. The 14th Company had very successful seasons in all three of these sports. It was obviously not comparable to playing at varsity level. My disillusionment with allowing politics to play a part in selecting the best athletes prevented me from trying out for either the soccer or squash varsity teams. As an ironic aftermath, I received a phone call in 2001 asking me to contribute to a going-away gift for Navy's 'grand old man of baseball:' Joe Duff. Duff was retiring after 40 years. After sharing my youngster year experience with the solicitor, he quickly hung up the phone.

June Week was the last week of the academic year and it consisted of five or so days of dances and parties before summer cruises.

About five or six of us rented a house where all the June Week dates slept. It turned into a yearly event with Larry Smith, Duke Edwards, Jake Oaks, Hal Dolenga, Hoppy Hohenstein, Hal Moore and me participating. Virtually every couple in the house ended up getting married in June 1956. It looked like true love.

Two classes (first and third) deployed on ships while the new second classmen were introduced to aviation and amphibious warfare. The two-month second class summer program was mostly fun and the specialized branches of the Navy and Marine Corps did their best to entice the best and brightest midshipmen to sign up for their specialty, although actual selection occurred first class year. About a quarter of my class joined the Air Force, which always seemed a bit strange to me. The Naval Academy had four years to 'sell' the Navy to a group of highly motivated, mission oriented, type A, over-achievers. Yet, just a minority of graduates was interested in going to sea. Ten percent joined the Marine Corps and as many who could pass the flight physical chose to fly. The most common reason for disqualifying flight candidates was poor eyesight.

As part of second class summer, trips to the Naval Air Test Center at Patuxent River, Maryland were quite exciting for those midshipmen who had any desire to fly or to pursue a career in aviation. For others, who got air sick, it was just another unpleasant experience in their quest to find a suitable career choice. The life of an 'Airedale' certainly appeared to be superior to that of a SEAL or a marine storming the beach in amphibious warfare. The only decision I think I made that summer was not to go to flight training directly from the Academy. My logic was that to be promoted to admiral and eventually Chief of Naval Operations, it would be advantageous to be both a 'black shoe' (surface officer) to understand shipboard operations, and a 'brown shoe' (aviator).

Summer leave came with 50 percent of my Academy training and education competed. It was uneventful, splitting time between Doylestown and Northumberland. Hitchhiking to and from was quite easy in the 1950s and a common means of cheap transport. Will had just completed his prep school year and was off to Annapolis.

Each succeeding year at USNA got easier for me. Russian was behind me and I was adjusting quite well to professional subjects. Aptitude for the service (grease) also kicked in with a higher weighting factor in computing overall grades and I scored quite high in grease (3.79 out of 4.0 first class year). Our company officer was a decorated Marine Corps Captain (Robert D. Whitesell), who was nicknamed 'Nails' by everyone in the brigade. He took me aside several times trying to convince me to become a marine. I didn't reject his advice to his face, but there was no way I was going to sign up for the Marine Corps.

Will came in as a plebe during my second class year so I got to know quite a few of his classmates in the 18th Company. As usual, nothing seemed to faze him and he had a relatively easy first year. He caught for the plebe baseball team and played plebe basketball but did not start. It was undoubtedly easier to have an upper class brother in the brigade to help with professional questions and be part of his support network. Many midshipmen in the ruling class tended to give a break to younger brothers of classmates.

One other aspect of my third year at the Academy was a week-long trip to the U.S. Military Academy (USMA) at West Point as part of an exchange program. It was not so much fun as it was interesting. My observations, based upon five days, were that they stressed the physical side more than Navy. Their honor system required you to report any violation observed, not just your own missteps. And they encouraged competition to the point that students sat next to the person that was just below them and just above them in that given class. Any concept of teamwork clearly took a back seat to defeating your classmates. The cadets clearly marched better, and because they were assigned to companies based on their height, they looked much smarter at football game march-ons. Cadets seemed to be much more 'gung-ho' about being commissioned as second Lieutenants in the Army than the average midshipman was about his commissioning. Despite that, I am very pleased that I was accepted at Navy instead of the Military Academy.

First class cruise was a Mediterranean and British Isles deployment on board the battleship USS New Jersey. The 12-inch guns on the New Jersey were even more impressive than a cruiser's eight-inch main battery. During one practice firing at sea, the admiral's driver forgot to lower the windows of his sedan that was parked on deck. The under-pressure created by the big guns collapsed the car's roof as if a giant hand had crushed it. The Admiral was unhappy but the midshipmen were amused. I continued to emcee at midshipman happy hours as well as perform stand-up routines. There was no easier audience to work than one on board a ship.

We docked at Portsmouth, England, for about a week and I took the opportunity to take a London tour. I ran into a classmate who remarked that he had seen my brother and was attending a stage play with him that evening. I arranged a meeting with Wilbur that night after his show and we had an unexpected rendezvous, catching up on his cruise adventures.

Our second port of call was Barcelona, Spain, and my expectations for fun were much lower than in the UK, where language was no barrier. I accepted an invitation to the local tennis club and had a marvelous time with an attractive tennis-playing senorita, who took me under her wing. This was my first among many encounters with tennis players and they have never disappointed. I found that a sport that allows the opponent to be the sole arbiter in assigning points (i.e. judging whether balls are in or out) to be very appealing.

During that last leave in the summer of 1955, I learned that several more Doylestown residents were scheduled to be sworn in at the Naval Academy; Skip Yerkes, Ron Denney, Lee Robinson and Ducky Peters. I am not sure what I started in 1952 but with six midshipmen from a town of 5,000 people, this surely must have been a record. Five of the six would subsequently graduate with only one failing an English course and dropping out.

My final year at the Academy was, by far, the best. I was selected to be a 'two striper' by my classmates, which entailed being in charge of one platoon of the 14th company and being responsible for their military bearing. I was in contention for being selected midshipman company commander, but I had irritated several of my classmates with personal, sarcastic comments and they retaliated by grading me quite low in aptitude for the service. I was also chosen to be the Humor Editor of The Splinter, a monthly midshipman magazine that highlighted a lot of the informal aspects of life in Bancroft Hall. I led several football pep rallies, and in general became fairly well known around the campus.

My assigned plebe was a young man from Quakertown, Pennsylvania, which was just 10 miles from Doylestown. His name was Ed Gross and he was not only a quick study, but had all the characteristics that we were looking for in a midshipman. He had a fairly easy plebe year and I was glad to be of assistance in that transition phase of his life.

Over the Christmas holiday, the president of the Doylestown Kiwanis Club, Russ Thomas, (sports writer for the Intelligencer newspaper) invited all the local midshipmen to one of their weekly meetings. We presented a short program of what it was like to attend the Naval Academy. All six of us were featured in the local paper along with an article highlighting how unusual it was for so many midshipmen to be from one small town. I am sure there were many parents, as well as Sister Wilma, who were as proud as could be of their charges.

Spring arrived and with it the selection of services. I chose a destroyer home-ported in Pearl Harbor, Hawaii. In April I received orders to report not later than August 27, 1956. There is something omnipotent about military orders ("Upon graduation, you will regard yourself detached from duty at the USNA and will proceed to San Francisco, CA and report to the Commandant, Twelfth Naval District, for transportation to the USS Radford (DDE 446) and upon arrival report to the commanding officer of that vessel for duty"). By that time I was savvy enough to know not to knock on the Commandant's front door and inquire about a flight to Hawaii.

With official orders in hand and a firm wedding date decided, graduation was almost anti-climatic. The anchorman in the class, Jim

Visage, was from my company. Since we sat alphabetically for graduation, my picture appeared in most national newspapers hoisting Visage on our shoulders. Why there is such interest in the anchorman I'm not sure. I would much prefer to have graduated 520 (out of 681) than dead last. There was an award for the midshipman whose grades improved the most from plebe to first-class year and I thought I had a chance to win since my first year grades had been fairly low. But Pete Randrup was announced as the winner.

Looking back at those four years, I concluded I changed from a provincial idealist with no clue about the opposite sex to an urban world traveler, still with no clue about the opposite sex. I was counting on marriage to end that shortcoming. A second observation was that plebe training did an effective job of desensitizing one's emotions. After world class criticism for a prolonged period of time, the inner spirit builds a thick protective skin that sheds all derogatory comments. Development of this characteristic was useful in high stress situations, but it didn't do much for the new age sensitive male persona that was expected to empathize with the opposite sex.

Many midshipmen had great difficulty adjusting to military discipline. They often took criticism personally. My experience at Tabor Home allowed me to transition to a military life very easily. I had already accepted the premise that life wasn't fair and that a tenacious spirit was more valuable in life than intelligence. And I never took disparaging comments personally. School was over and my career was about to start. Life was exciting!

CHAPTER 6

Life as a Black Shoe

Live within your income, even if you have to borrow to do so.

OF ALL OF the possible methods that could be used to assign newly commissioned Naval Academy trained ensigns to billets in the fleet, the one that I would not choose is assignment by lottery, but that is exactly how your initial assignment was established. Regardless of class standing, you were assigned to your first duty station by the number you drew out of a hat during first class year. My number was 44, which meant I could go immediately to flight training, join the Marine Corps, or get any type of ship based any place in the country.

With my long range goal of becoming Chief of Naval Operations driving my thinking, my initial plan was to spend one or two years in destroyers before applying for flight training. Newport, Rhode Island seemed like an interesting port for several reasons. It was more appealing than Norfolk, Virginia, a typical navy town that had a reputation for being inhospitable to Navy personnel. (A local newspaper once ran a picture showing a sign posted near the naval station that read "All dogs and sailors keep off the grass.") Pictures of the beautiful Newport historic mansions on the hills overlooking the Atlantic Ocean were very impressive. You can quickly see the lack of any meaningful analysis associated with planning my naval career.

Just days before selection, I overheard George Biles, a classmate who lived next door in Bancroft Hall, extolling the virtues of destroyer duty at Pearl Harbor, Hawaii. He was uncertain whether his number was low enough to be selected but he was going to give it a shot. After a quick telephone call to my fiancée, Donna Sulouff, who was fine with the idea of living in Hawaii, I told George I had decided to request Pearl. His indignation with me subsided when he got the last destroyer available in Hawaii. As it turned out, we were in the same squadron and saw quite of bit of each other.

June 30,1956, the day of Donna and my wedding, turned out to be a beautiful summer day in central Pennsylvania, which was fortunate since our nuptials were scheduled outdoors. Brother Will was my best man and he looked splendid in his dress white uniform. In addition to rounding up relatives and friends to attend our wedding, a number of Tabor children drove out to Northumberland, Pennsylvania, as did Sister Wilma. She must have thought: "Now here is a marriage made in heaven. What could be better than the joining of two nice Lutherans raised with strong religious beliefs? No doubt this union will be long-lasting." Unfortunately, subsequent events proved such idealistic thoughts were wrong.

The wedding trip was a long one, consisting of driving cross country to visit my sister Jean in Chicago, as well as some long lost aunts and uncles on my mother's side in Dallas, Clovis, NM, and San Francisco. It was always very enjoyable to see my sister even though I spent so little time with her growing up. She always had a joke to share and she viewed life as a comedy. She would never be selected by the editors of Home Beautiful to feature her house but she was a loving mother who always had time to still a fear or kiss an injured knee.

Regarding my mother's siblings, I thought it unusual that the only relative who ever made any attempt at communicating with me during my childhood years was my Aunt Helen Brewer. All my newly found aunts, uncles and cousins were engaging and interesting people but I was saddened after our brief visit to realize that it was up to me to pursue any future relationship with them. My peripatetic lifestyle in the Navy did not lend itself to maintaining a long distance relationship with relatives who showed no great interest in my life or well-being. With the exception of Aunt Helen, I never heard from any of the Dorris clan again.

Our wedding trip ended in San Francisco. Dependents were not permitted to travel to any overseas duty station until family housing was obtained. I dropped Donna off in San Diego, at the home of my Naval Academy roommate Hoppy Hohenstein's parents. I flew the 2,000 miles to Honolulu to report to the destroyer *Radford*, which was undergoing a major overhaul in a Pearl Harbor dry dock.

After checking into the bachelor officers' quarters on the base, I started the long process of attempting to become an effective naval officer. The gunnery officer, Lt. H.O. Mains, who was a bachelor, took me under his wing. On weekends he taught me how to surfboard on the pristine beaches at Barber's Point Naval Air Station. It took about 24 hours of surfing before I could consistently stand on the board. It became an enjoyable pastime after mastering that basic step.

Meanwhile, I requested base housing so I could get on with married life. It took two months, but finally my number came up and in November, Donna was to arrive and we could move into 123 Main Street in Naval Housing Area Number 1. Our house was a one bedroom structure just a block from the main entrance of Pearl Harbor Naval Station. Block Arena, a huge amphitheater where basketball games were played and visiting dignitaries like Bob Hope would perform, was located directly across the street.

On the day Donna was scheduled to catch the plane to Honolulu, she couldn't get organized in time to leave for the airport. So the plane arrived in Hawaii without her. She was never a slave to a clock and maintained that disdain for punctuality our entire married life. I had some difficulty adjusting to this foible, but she made connections on the next scheduled flight and found life on Oahu much to her liking. We shipped her 1951 Ford to the Islands and commenced married life.

My base salary was $222 a month, ($2063 in 2019 dollars) which was a livable wage in 1956, as long as a large car payment was not

59

part of the budget. That might not seem like much by today's standards, but with no housing costs and living on the small Island of Oahu, our expenses were easily contained. By no housing expenses, I meant just that. Base housing employees would even come to your home to replace a burned out light bulb.

The *Radford* completed its yard overhaul and we started daily operations in December in preparation for a February deployment to the Western Pacific via Australia. For a brand new ensign, this was high adventure. The advantage of the ship's operating area being so close to port was twofold. We seldom stayed out overnight and the junior officers received marvelous training in maneuvering the ship in the channel and docking along side the pier. One of the other ensigns, an NROTC graduate named Ken Burns, disliked being under the watchful eye of the CO (commanding officer), so he offered his scheduled Officer of the Deck (OOD) periods to me. I couldn't believe anyone would not like maneuvering and docking a destroyer. I found the entire crew very professional and dedicated. The CO, Commander Bud Woodson (USNA '42), was especially inspiring. He enjoyed every day at sea and shared his tales of World War II.

After a very short period in the engineering department on board *Radford*, I was transferred to the gunnery department and became the Anti-Submarine Warfare (ASW), as well as the Fire Control (weapons), Officer. My department operated the SONAR (equipment that transmits sound into the water and records the positions of objects based on the reflected return) and maintained the weapon systems that control both the guns and the anti-submarine weapons. It was an ideal training ground for a brand new ensign. The ship's primary mission was to track and kill enemy submarines with depth charges and hedgehogs. Depth charges are weapons that are dropped off surface ships and detonated at a pre-set depth, such as 150 feet. A hedgehog is fired off a deck mounted pod and is detonated by striking the hull of the submarine. They are shot in clusters to increase the probability of striking a moving target. Neither of these weapons is used in today's Navy.

Here is a general truth that you will not hear from many married naval officers; it is fun to go to sea. Some situations are more fun than others; it is obviously more fun in calm seas than in stormy weather. It is more fun flying helicopters from carriers than standing midwatches (midnight until 4 A.M.) on destroyers. It is more fun visiting Hong Kong than having shore leave in Subic Bay in the Philippines. Being underway and accomplishing an interesting mission with Navy people who are upbeat, dedicated and amusing, is quite satisfying. There are no bills to pay, no children to discipline, no cars that break down, no household chores, no garbage to take out and no justification required for watching football games on Sundays. In short, you get credit for keeping the world safe for democracy while avoiding many of the required tasks of life.

Life was not easy on a small combatant ship. We usually stood two four-hour watches per day on the bridge (station from which the ship is commanded) or in the Combat Information Center (CIC) right behind the bridge. One of those four hour watches would be at night. Sleeping was not permitted during the working day (except on Sunday) so everyone was in a perpetual sleep deprived state. It normally takes from six to 12 months to qualify as Officer of the Deck Underway (ability to control the ship's position in the task force), depending on how many days the ship was at sea during the year. I qualified in the minimum amount of time and felt very competent in all phases of destroyer operations. Maneuvering with a task force at night was especially challenging and rewarding. Solving a maneuvering board problem at the Academy was a chore. Finding a rapid solution at sea was enjoyable.

On the *Radford* and on every other U.S. combat ship, each member of the officer's mess contributes an equal amount toward the cost of the food that is served in the wardroom (dining room) both underway and in port. In the late 1950s, the average cost of food per officer came to $30 a month during deployments. When there was a full complement of officers at evening meal, a 'buck' (small statue with a heavy base) was rotated daily. The position of the buck denoted who would be served first during that meal. It signified the social equality of each member of the mess. It reinforced the one member, one vote concept when expending funds that belong to the mess. Hence, a guest of an individual member was literally a guest of the entire wardroom.

This precept made such an impression on me as a junior officer that I decided to institute that tradition in my own family. Each family member would be treated as a social equal with regard to courtesy and dignity and would always be afforded the opportunity to voice his or her opinion. That meant that the channel to be watched on the one television set would be voted on, with the majority ruling. Trading votes for future considerations turned out to be a valuable lesson in mastering interpersonal relationships. Social equality did have some trying moments, such as the time I had to go to a neighbor's house to watch the Super Bowl, but such instances were rare. My children all developed high self-esteem and felt no need to outwit the system.

The Radford had one of the most effective ship borne SONAR systems in the fleet, the SQS-4. The distance that it could pick up a submarine target was classified, but our ASW team was quite proficient in detecting and classifying underwater contacts. The real shortcoming in the surface navy was destroying the enemy subs after they were correctly classified (properly identified).

Classification was no easy task since whale contacts look and sound similar to submarine targets. There were strict guidelines established before a surface ship or aircraft could attack an undersea target in combat. Two different sensors had to detect the unknown target and the contact had to sound and maneuver similar to a submarine. It was widely believed among U.S. submariners that their nemesis in combat would be friendly ASW forces that might be too quick to pull the trigger. We had an underwater telephone on the ship and the Soviets and U.S. forces had agreed on code words to use in the event we encountered an unidentified submarine and wanted it to surface to avoid being attacked. Those were exciting days of the cold war.

With the advent of the high speed submarine in 1954, it became evident to me that the days of destroyers defeating the subsurface boats were numbered. I concluded that helicopters equipped with long range SONAR would be the only possible solution in combating high speed submarines since the hunted could now outrun and kill the surface ship hunters. This revelation would influence my decision on what type of aircraft to fly and to remain in Anti-Submarine Warfare.

My first deployment to the Western Pacific (West Pac) occurred early in 1957. I had no idea that would be the first of 10 West Pac cruises that I would complete over the next 16 years. The length of a West Pac cruise varied from six to seven months, which meant that I would spend over five years cruising on board ships in the Pacific Ocean.

Our first port of call was Pago Pago, the capital city of American Samoa. The local basketball team challenged those of us on the Radford to a game. We had an excellent team and quickly accepted, knowing that it would be no contest based on our height advantage of 12 inches per player. What we did not take into account was the weather 60 miles north of the equator at high noon. We jumped to a huge lead but watched forlornly as our team wilted in the oppressive heat. They literally ran us off the court in the second half.

We crossed the equator on March 18, 1957 and everyone was quite surprised that I was already a trusty shellback (a classification of those who had crossed the equator on a naval vessel.), even though I was only an ensign. There were only about 18 shellbacks on the whole ship. With so few paddle wielders and so many pollywogs (those who have not crossed the equator) to initiate, getting painful sunburn under the equatorial sky was more likely to cause discomfort than getting your backside reddened with homemade shillelaghs.

I was the in port OOD when the Radford tied up under the world renowned Sydney Bridge. Two events occurred that I was unprepared to handle. The first was a group of 'ban the bomb' marauders that bombarded our ship with bags of flour from the overhead bridge. We cleaned up the mess as quickly as possible. The same group acquired a small boat with the intent to paint their slogan on the side of our ship. I ordered the fire hoses to be used to discourage the marauders, but my efforts fell short. They managed to paint their slogan on our bow. Our ship's picture was on the front page of the Sydney Herald the next morning. The CO was not impressed with the bad publicity of seeing his ship in the news.

On our final day in port, I was OOD again. The ship had taken muster and all hands were present and accounted for. While we were still in the outbound channel, three enlisted men were reported missing. "Impossible," I said. "Nobody left the ship while I was on duty." As I later found out, one man had concealed himself in a trashcan and two of his buddies carried him off the ship. They had met three Australian lassies, fallen madly in love and decided they would spend the rest of their life on an Australian sheep ranch.

Within 24 hours one of the girls' parents reported the American lads to the local shore patrol, who arrested them and sent them back to the Radford. To add insult to injury, I was assigned as legal counsel to defend them at their court martial. They got thirty days in the brig on bread and water and had to pay all the travel expenses to get them back to the ship. So much for true love.

I made two observations about Aussies at the time. Nearly every Australian loved Americans and was grateful that the United States defended Australia from the Japanese during World War II. Secondly, probably all young Australian men did not have a clue how to treat women. Consequently, American sailors had an easy time of stealing the hearts of the young Australian damsels whenever a U.S. ship sailed into port.

Our next port was Sasebo, Japan. In 1957 there were still strong feelings in the United States regarding the empire of Japan. I had deep prejudices against both Germany and Japan based on the huge amount of propaganda that I had been exposed to during World War II. Photos of Japanese soldiers throwing babies in the air and bayoneting them had a lasting effect on many Americans. This bias was reinforced by the fact that one could smell Japan several hundred miles across the sea because of the open sewer ditches that crisscrossed the country.

No dollars were used for purchases on military bases in the Far East. The currency used on military establishments was MPC (military payment currency), which, on base, had an exchange rate of 360 yen to $1 MPC. The market rate in Japan was in excess of 400 yen to the U.S. greenback but this was the U.S. government's method of supporting the Japanese economy. You had to convert MPC dollars to yen at the Officers' club before proceeding out the gate. Many of the local bars would take MPC, illegally, and have their special friends within the U.S. Navy convert them back to yen. Periodically the base would call for a lock down and convert all old MPC to a new issue. When that occurred, all the Japanese nationals holding MPC would see their money become worthless overnight.

After a short exposure to the Japanese culture, I did a complete about face in my feelings toward Japan. It was the most courteous and honest society I could imagine. It was quite common for cabdrivers to return wallets full of money that had been left by mistake in their cabs. Fights between Japanese and Americans at any of the local bars were unusual. Cleanliness was highly cherished among the Japanese and they all took great pains not to offend the American guests visiting their country.

They did not get reciprocity. Americans felt superior to the Japanese people who were still feeling the effects of World War II. Enlisted men were prohibited from marrying Asian women without the permission of their commanding officer, who seldom granted their request. The Navy shore patrol kept a tight leash on sailors who had too much to drink, but bar owners were seldom compensated for furniture that was damaged by enthusiastic drinkers.

The first week in Sasebo I ran into a high school classmate, Dan Tomlinson. He was an ensign serving in the Navy Supply Corps. Dan was a funny iconoclast who was never serious about anything in life. I was shocked that Dan could pass a Navy physical since he was about 50 pounds overweight. He offered to show me the city after dinner in the Officers' club one evening. Against my better judgment, I agreed. After visiting several of his favorite bars, he led me to a geisha house and banged on the door. When the 'mama-san' (woman manager) opened the door, Dan requested to enter and take pictures of the proceedings. His request was immediately met with a loud declarative statement in broken English; "No cameras. No cameras." She then asked him to leave the premises and never return. Dan was greatly amused at the contrived incident.

The remainder of the cruise was spent conducting ASW operations with an accompanying U.S. submarine. The Radford spent most of her in-port time in the Japanese city of Yokusaka, about an hour's train ride from Tokyo. Almost no one visited the Japanese capital because of the high prices, noise, and crowded streets.

Bars in all navy towns were segregated as either for officers or enlisted men to minimize any socializing with alcohol. At the first indication of trouble by any American customer, the owner would call for the shore patrol, who would respond within minutes. If individual bars had too many fights or complaints, the Navy would place the establishment off-limits and, in effect, close it down.

'Working girls' (bar maids) had monthly physicals by U.S. Navy doctors to ensure they were free of venereal disease (VD). It was understood that any officer who contracted VD could count on being passed over for his next promotion. The girls would make a living by getting customers to buy them alcoholic drinks (actually tea) until the benefactor's money was gone. Part of the game was trying to avoid the big-spending customer who expected more than a kiss on the cheek after the bar closed at midnight. In the 1950s, in Japan, western style clothing was uncommon. There was something very appealing about little Japanese girls dressed in kimonos, bowing and smiling as if their most pressing task was to make you feel important.

Although the Navy made valiant attempts to institute security among the troops regarding the movement of ships, bar girls were the first to know when and if a ship's schedule had changed. They had reliable sources (often senior officers) and were invariably correct.

Yokosuka and Sasebo were the primary ports of call in Japan but occasionally there were other destinations that proved interesting; Nara, Osaka, Kobe, and Kyoto. They were all in the southern portions of Honshu (the largest of the four major islands) and were among the most beautiful and serene sections of the country.

At least once on each deployment, the ship would visit the British Crown Colony, Hong Kong. It was, without a doubt, the favorite liberty port of all Navy men. The shopping bargains were spectacular, the made-to-measure suits were of high quality and affordable, and the exchange rate ensured that you received the best value for your money. If you didn't like shopping, you could take a cable car up the mountain and view the harbor, or you could ride the ferry or a water taxi to Kowloon. There were interesting options for tourists such as dining on a floating restaurant or visiting a pottery factory or a pearl farm. Hong Kong was really a magical place.

Returning from six or seven month deployments was a joyous occasion. There was an infectious thrill of sighting home after many months away and seeing waving hands from family and friends at pier side. The sound of the Navy band could send chills through even the most insensitive returnee. There were gifts to distribute, stories to tell, and appreciation of wives and families that people who share lives on a daily basis do not experience. Although divorce rates among navy couples were higher than the norm, there were some whose marriage actually lasted longer because of the forced separation for extended periods of time.

Several months after my first cruise, Donna and I had an event that would change our lifestyle forever. Stephen was born in October 1957 and turned out to be the perfect child. Since I was scheduled to start flight training in a little more than a year, we decided not to request a two bedroom house, so Steve was the only child in the entire housing complex of childless couples. He was the center of attention whenever Donna took him outside the house and he loved all the fussing. His broad smiles and unintelligible murmurings seemed to charm his audience. We spent a small fortune on baby pictures that we sent off to every friend and relative in our address book.

During the autumn of 1957, the Pearl Harbor Navy basketball team, the Bluejackets, had tryouts for its upcoming 24 game season in the University-Armed Forces Conference. The reason it was looking for players was its record in 1956; one win and twenty three losses. They had the league's scoring leader in Jack Bradbury from Brigham Young University but not much else. The team also hired an experienced Hawaiian coach, Chew Chong Ching. Four players from the Radford tried out and both Larry Magner (USNA '57 varsity player) and I started for the Bluejackets. We didn't have a spectacular year but managed to win seven or eight contests. Jack Bradbury again led the league in scoring and I averaged 13 points a game. Not bad for a guy playing against division one college ballplayers. It reinforced my belief that I could play with the big boys of college basketball. We defeated the University of Hawaii and several pretty good service teams that season, including a local team starring five foot seven Chuck Rolles. He was raised in Binghamton, NY and played for Cornell in Ithaca. Several polls selected him as an All American first team player, so we were excited to compete against him. Not only did we defeat his team, but I outscored him! (Chuck died in October 2018 at age 84 and the Binghamton paper had a big write up in the obituary section.)

A normal deployment cycle was six months at sea and one year between cruises. The 12 months in port was necessary to train new crewmembers both individually and in teams, maintain and upgrade shipboard equipment, and complete professional correspondence courses such as navigation and gunnery.

Hawaii was also a nice place to recharge your batteries after an arduous at sea period. Beaches were free and the weather was boringly spectacular, sunny every day with an afternoon rain shower that the locals called pineapple juice. The Officers' club was inexpensive and the dining was first class. The drive around Oahu took about five or six hours and the views were breathtaking. We hosted no relatives or close friends because people didn't travel much in the late 1950s. The idyllic existence was coming to a close after a second West Pac cruise that began in April 1958.

Several memorable events took place during that deployment. The first was an opportunity to be transferred to the USS Philippine Sea via high line, which is a passenger basket on a wire (similar to a clothesline) that is secured on ships at both ends. The Phil Sea was an anti-submarine carrier that carried both fixed wing and rotary wing aircraft to prosecute enemy submarines. The admiral initiated an exchange program within the task force to familiarize destroyer officers with carriers and vice versa. The visiting officer was exposed to the Combat Information Center and the bridge of the host ship. It was designed to create better understanding among members of the task force. I was transferred to the carrier after dark and was escorted immediately to a stateroom. In short order I was out like a light since all destroyer officers were sleep deprived.

My next memory was being awakened by soft, high fidelity music, which turned out to be my new roommate's stereo equipment. I thought I had arrived in heaven. The contrast between life on a destroyer that rolls ten degrees left and right during relatively calm seas, and that of a carrier, where one is awakened by heavenly stereo music, was shocking. If I ever had any reservations about joining the Airedale (aviation) Navy before that trip, they were quickly overcome. It seemed incredible that sea duty on a carrier was so much more enjoyable than on a destroyer, and the Navy paid you more money just to fly their aircraft. (Someone pointed out that the Navy doesn't pay aviators more money; they just pay it sooner.)

A second incident involved a curious tradition that was established among ships of the Pacific fleet in the late 1950s. A signed picture of a movie star was presented to the wardroom of one of the ships. It was prominently displayed and was the pride of the ship's officers. It disappeared one day and the gloom that resulted transformed into anger when it was discovered that a sister ship had stolen the treasure. When a third ship heard the story, their officer corps developed a plan to relieve the wardroom of their ill-gotten treasure. And so a Pacific wide tradition (stealing the framed picture) was established.

The *Radford* became involved by chance. Our First Lieutenant, Lieutenant (junior grade) Ira Riskin, was visiting the *Philippine Sea* on official business at sea when the ship went to general quarters. Everyone was required to report to a battle station, leaving Ira alone in the wardroom. He immediately removed the prize and stored it under his jacket. He was hoping the theft would not be discovered before he was high lined back to his destroyer. It was not discovered and he was greeted on the *Radford* as a conquering hero. The first night the *Radford* came alongside the *Phil Sea* for reprovisioning, a flag was hoisted from the yardarm indicating we were in possession of the picture. The shouted insults and expletives from the *Phil Sea* could be heard a hundred yards away.

Arriving back in our home port, Pearl Harbor, the officers were careful to guard our newly acquired guest. We told a brand new officer who just reported on board, Ensign Ron Murphy, the details of the heist. He seemed proud to be joining such an enterprising ship's company. Several days later at midnight, Ensign 'Murphy' contacted the *O'Bannon*, a sister ship, by flashing light informing them to take action. A small boat full of *O'Bannon* officers pulled along side *Radford* and overpowered the two officers on duty and made off with the beloved picture. The turncoat, who turned out not to be Ensign Murphy, but an officer that had just reported for duty on *O'Bannon*, was punished by shaving his head bald and sending him back to his ship. The real Ensign Murphy reported for duty a week later and wondered why the ship's officers were so hostile for the first few days.

My brother graduated in June of 1958 along with about 800 classmates. I think our Dad was more proud of having two sons graduate from the Naval Academy than anything he had accomplished in his lifetime. Will wasn't the anchorman but there were only about five names separating him from that dubious honor. His poor eyesight precluded him from flying so he signed up for Air Force ground (non-flying).

With orders to Pensacola, Florida, in hand, Donna, Stephen, and I flew back to the East Coast in early November to spend Christmas in Pennsylvania to show off our 14-month-old child. The flight back was uneventful with the exception of my paying insufficient attention to baby Steve. I stood him on the airplane seat before strapping him in, and as I was putting some hand luggage in the overhead compartment, he toppled to the floor, headfirst. I would like to officially record this incident, so that in the event of any future strange behavior by Stephen, there will be some logical explanation.

After a 15-day leave period, I caught an overnight train to Pensacola to commence ground school, which is conducted before actually flying, and arrange for housing for Donna and Steve. I was unsure how difficult flight training would be but I was convinced it could not be any harder than life as a black shoe on a destroyer.

CHAPTER 7

Wings of Gold

*A good landing is one you can walk away from and
a really great one is when you can use the airplane again.*

THERE WAS A plaque for sale in the Navy Exchange written by a local fifth grade boy, entitled "I Want to Be a Pilot" it read:

"I want to be a pilot when I grow up because it's fun and easy to do. Pilots don't need much school; they just have to learn numbers so they can read instruments. I guess they should be able to read maps so they can find their way if they get lost. Pilots should be brave so they won't get scared if it's foggy and they can't see, or if a wing or motor falls off. They should stay calm so they'll know what to do. Pilots have to have good eyes so they can see through clouds and they can't be afraid of lightning or thunder because they are closer to them than we are. The salary pilots make is another thing I like. They make more money than they can spend. This is because most people think airplane flying is dangerous except pilots don't because they know how easy it is. There isn't much I don't like, except girls like pilots and all the stewardesses want to marry them and they always have to chase them away so they won't bother them. I hope I don't get airsick because if I do, I couldn't be a pilot and would have to go to work."

Armed with not much more knowledge about being a pilot than the anonymous fifth grader, I reported into the Naval Air Training

Center, Pensacola, Florida, ready to take on the challenge of winning wings of gold.

Pensacola is a city with 50,000 inhabitants located on the panhandle of Florida. It has trained pilots since 1914 so it is definitely a Navy town. About half of the wives of naval aviators met their husbands when they were undergoing flight training in Pensacola. It is an idyllic setting on the Gulf of Mexico and adjacent to miles of sandy beaches. It was there in November of 1958 that I started the 18 month quest to become a naval aviator.

Pilot candidates were recruited from three major sources: newly commissioned officers, fleet experienced officers and Naval Cadets (NavCads). Officers from the fleet were a small percentage and had the highest washout rate. NavCads were generally the best stick and throttle aviators but some of them failed to pass the ground portion of flight training. The washout rate varied by the needs of the fleet, but on average about 30 percent of those entering training failed to get their wings. (During the latter portions of the Vietnam War, virtually no one washed out.)

I bumped into Jack Apple at the Bachelor Officers' Quarters (BOQ) on my first day in Pensacola. He was a bright, slightly overweight, non athletic classmate from my company (14th) at the Academy and I had known him for four years. We could not have been more different in our background, outlook, and value systems. Jack's father was a wealthy businessman from Philadelphia and he had a privileged upbringing. We were never friendly at boat school (slang for the Naval Academy) for a variety of reasons. He had just washed out of the flight program and was awaiting reassignment to the surface fleet. I had never seen a more humble and defeated naval officer, quite uncharacteristic for Jack. Despite our past conflicts, I felt great compassion for him since he had just faced his first major obstacle in his short career and failed to clear it. (He applied to sub school a year later and subsequently had a very successful career under the sea.)

The naval flight training program consisted of two months of ground school followed by 50 flight hours in a primary trainer aircraft

(T-34B). Successful student pilots then traveled to Whiting Field for training in the T-28, a high performance single engine propeller aircraft with more power than any fighter in World War II. Following that, the class was divided into several pipelines for advanced training in jets, patrol aircraft, carrier-based props and helicopters. If all went well, the students would earn their wings in eighteen months and accrue 200 flight hours. Some would be dropped from the program for performance reasons. A few would initiate the request themselves. All would remember the experience.

Here is a quick word about the degree of difficulty in flying aircraft. Anyone with average intelligence and coordination is capable of flying safely. It does not take nerves of steel or the skill of a collegiate athlete. The reason for the relatively high dropout rate among military student aviators is the time factor. An arbitrary decision was made to maintain the standard of a certain level of progress that equated to the average student being qualified to solo in 24 flight hours with 35 practice landings. For those few who were unable to solo in that time frame, a decision would be made to determine how much more practice time would be allotted for them to qualify. In most cases, one or two more flights would be awarded and the check pilot would certify that the student was now capable of reaching the safe-for-solo milestone.

A building blocks approach is used acquiring further piloting skills such as in acrobatics, formation flying, carrier landing, instrument flying, and air-to-air combat. Students vary in their skill level of mastering newly introduced piloting techniques. I personally found instrument flying easier to master than basic stick and rudder visual flying. Being prepared for each flight and demonstrating a satisfactory level of knowledge to the instructor pilot on a daily basis was the key to successfully navigating the maze called naval flight training.

Of course, everyone has a bad day now and then. You can't have too many of these days during flight training or you end up back in the surface fleet driving ships instead of aircraft.

Ground school required some long hours of study since much of the vocabulary in aviation was new. The T-34B aircraft systems had to be understood in depth. In addition, the location of every instrument, gauge, switch, lever and button in the cockpit had to be memorized and its function understood. Engine performance and aircraft limitations were other subjects to be studied and absorbed. Emergency procedures were important and there was no room for error in spouting off the precise procedures to follow in the event a system had failed or malfunctioned.

Another aspect of flight training is the preparation necessary in the event things don't go according to plan. It is entirely possible that an aviator will end up in the water sometime during an extended period of flying over it. To prepare pilots for such an event, familiarization with parachutes, as well as escaping from a submerged cockpit, are necessary skills. The Naval Air Training Command incorporated simulated parachute jumping, removal of the chute while being dragged in the water, and extricating oneself from a Dilbert Dunker. The latter is a realistic cockpit mounted on a pair of runners that dives into the pool and turns upside down with the trainee strapped in. The strategy is to wait until the bubbles clear, release the harness and find your way to the surface. It seems like an eternity when you are in the water, inverted, but the whole maneuver takes about 30 seconds. A few participants have difficulty escaping so the dunker operator reverses the process and restores the machine to its original position at the top of the slide. Safety divers are in the pool to assist in the event of an emergency. The second time down is always successful.

In the dynamic world of Navy flight training, a set number of qualified aviators are expected to appear for fleet assignment 18 months after their enrollment date. In addition to this broad requirement for pilots, each specialty branch must fill the vacancies that occur during that time frame. Consequently, there are constant changes in the number of required jet pilots or patrol pilots in any given month. If you produce too many, you have aviators sitting around with no aircraft to fly. Produce too few and you have overtaxed pilots flying more than a safe number of missions per week.

Just as my preflight class was entering the pipeline, it was discovered there were too many instructor pilots teaching carrier landings. A decision was made to transfer one squadron of instructors from carrier to basic training in the T-34Bs. I am sure that was undesirable from a student's viewpoint since, after the first month, the failure rate in my class (number of unsatisfactory flights or 'downs') was about double that of other classes. A top level review highlighted the situation and it was subsequently corrected but not before several candidates were washed out of the program. Expectations of instructors accustomed to students in the carrier phase of training were much higher than the skills demonstrated by beginning students.

An explanation of the evaluation system used in flight training might assist the reader in understanding the results. Each check flight in an airplane or simulator consists of ten to fifteen events, which are graded average, above average, below average or unsatisfactory. In addition, a category called 'headwork' (ability to solve in flight problems) was always evaluated. A student can receive a down (failing grade) for an unsatisfactory procedure or an excessive number of below averages. The system is not the most objective, but it has worked for decades with reasonable results. It assumes instructors are standardized in recognizing average performance and that they do not have a bias while grading. I recall one instructor telling me about grading his very first student. The instructor demonstrated the maneuver. The student then flew it about as well as the instructor, who considered himself an average fleet pilot. So he graded the student average. The instructor said he did not realize for some time that his first student was far and away the best student he had ever seen. Yet, he ended up evaluating him as average.

My pre-solo flights were fairly uneventful and I was quite impressed with my assigned instructor, Lt. Dwyer. He was a seasoned fleet pilot and very little ruffled his quiet demeanor. My first crisis happened on flight A-12 (12th flight in the syllabus) when I received a 'down' (unsatisfactory flight) from Lt(jg) Nelson, the check pilot. I recall it, not only because all flight failures are memorable, but also because I flew a good hop (a successful flight). It became obvious during the flight that his purpose was to establish the fact that he was the boss even though we were both the same rank. His arrogance really rankled me and I made a mental note to remember to be wary of officers like Nelson in the future. I was awarded two extra practice sessions and reflew the check flight that resulted in my clearance to solo on April 15, 1959.

Navy journalists assigned to the training command were always looking for unique stories. After all, how interesting is an article about a student flying by himself for the first time? It happens every single day in Pensacola. But, if the pilot flying the solo is named Orville Wright, then that is a human interest story. My photo and a short article were put out on the Associated Press wire service, which was sent out all over the country.

Although it was usually positive to have a famous name, there were occasional drawbacks. Before one flight, the instructor told me he hoped I would fly a bad hop that day. Surprised at such a comment, I inquired why? His reply was, "I would like nothing better that to tell my grandchildren that I was responsible for washing out Orville Wright from flight school." I assumed he was joking.

Throughout the year and a half training period I found nearly every instructor competent and interested in passing on his knowledge to the student. There was generally a sense of camaraderie in the cockpit rather than a typical professor-student relationship. Despite that positive environment, every student pilot was always aware that they were just a few unsatisfactory hops away from career failure.

Check flight B-18 (final flight in the T-34 trainer) was successfully flown during the first week in May and I was off to Whiting Field, an auxiliary airfield about 20 miles north of Pensacola. That would be my home for the next four months flying the single engine T-28 while learning acrobatics, formation flying, cross-country techniques, and carrier landings/takeoffs. I was assigned to Class 5B-S along with 29 other students from various backgrounds, who had survived the initial hurdle. As I view the roster, some 47 years later, I recognize few names. Ten are listed as naval or marine cadets (two year college graduates), 16 are ensigns (four-year college graduates), two are Cuban midshipmen, and one is a marine first lieutenant. I was the assigned section leader since I held the distinguished rank of lieutenant (junior grade). At least six of the class did not survive Whiting for a variety of reasons, including being dropped at their own request.

I recall Harold Botkins, an ensign from the U.S. Coast Guard. In an informal discussion in the Ready Room one day, he discussed one of his pet peeves. It was drivers who refused to lower their high beams while driving at night. His secret wish was to own a car made of lead, and drive it head-on into the offending driver. I was relived never to see his name in the national news describing such an accident. The only other class member that I can recall was Wade Simpson, only because his wife was quite attractive. I wonder if the remaining members of Class 5B-S remember as little as I do about our class?

My assigned instructor was Lt. Bernie Minetti and I felt fortunate since he was a squadron test pilot and knowledgeable about all aspects of the airplane. After eight familiarization and basic flying flights, I was cleared to fly solo with twelve hours of T-28 time under my belt. Solo flights were always enjoyable since there was no outside pressure to fly to a specified standard. It was always prudent to conduct the prescribed practice maneuvers since a check pilot later in the syllabus would evaluate your mastery of them.

On my fourth solo flight I was practicing touch-and-go landings at an outlying field. I failed to see and give way to another aircraft in the pattern. I learned of my indiscretion shortly after landing when Lt. Freund, a senior instructor pilot, intercepted me on the way back to the Ready Room and informed me of my shortcoming. Since he took no other action, I foolishly thought the incident was closed. The very next day he met me as I reported to work and told me to meet him at the airplane immediately after morning quarters. "Don't dally," he urged. I surmised that this flight was not going to be the highlight of my day.

From the outset it was obvious there was no possible way I could fly an 'up' check flight. In fact, I flew one of the best acrobatic hops (flights) in my short flying career but, because of the subjective nature of the grading system, any instructor could legitimately give a down to even Charles Lindbergh or John Glenn. About half way through the flight, Lt. Freund took control of the aircraft and flew us back to base. The debrief consisted of going down the checklist starting with the preflight and stating "unsat" after each item. It took all of 30 seconds to complete and we both knew this didn't have much to do with the flight I had just flown.

When Lt. Bernie Minetti found out I had received a down, he asked which maneuvers I had trouble with. When I demonstrated each airborne procedure for him, he was furious that they had been graded unsatisfactory. I know he met with Lt. Freund, even though it was fruitless, to get an explanation. For his concern, I have always had a warm spot in my heart for Bernie. He later joined me in my helicopter squadron, HS-2, after transitioning to helicopters.

The remaining T-28 syllabus went according to plan during the next three months. I did get to fly a formation hop with a childhood friend from Buckingham, Pennsylvania, Bucky DeVries. He had finished flight training and was immediately ordered to Whiting Field as an instructor. He also took me, along with a flight of four other student pilots, cross-country to New Orleans over a weekend. I recall making a less than stellar touchdown at the Naval Air Station as I stalled the aircraft over the numbers, several feet above the runway. Fortunately it resulted in just a hard landing but no damage.

The final phase of intermediate training consisted of two weeks of intense field-carrier-landing practice (flown to a runway that simulated a carrier deck) that culminated in six arrested (using a tail hook to land) carrier landings for the final exam. The syllabus of 18 sorties (individual flights) was designed to indoctrinate the student to follow the directions of the LSO (Landing Signal Officer) implicitly, without reservation or hesitation. During those two weeks of training, I am convinced I would have flown the airplane into the ship's superstructure if the LSO had directed it. It was the nearest thing to brainwashing that I have ever encountered. Directions were to be instantaneously followed without any thought-processing involved. Over 100 practice landings were accomplished in a small racetrack pattern that simulated the flight path to be flown around the carrier at sea. Flying the pattern in a precise manner became second nature. We were ready.

A pilot's first carrier landing ranks right behind his first solo in the list of memorable events. For most student pilots, it is the first time they have ever been on an aircraft carrier. The moving deck appears quite small when viewed from a cockpit several miles away. In addition, the movement of the ship through the water is deceptive since it appears to be moving quite rapidly when you are flying in the opposite direction (downwind) but it slows dramatically during the final approach into the wind line. Once the flight of four students led by an instructor was established in a holding pattern several miles away from the ship, cockpit canopies were opened as an added safety factor (for ease of escape) in the event of inadvertent water contact. (Aviators don't use crash.) The high wind noise makes radio communications difficult.

Our flight of four student pilots finally commenced our initial approach by flying up the starboard (right) side of the carrier before turning left across the bow and flying a parallel course in the opposite direction of the ship. As the aircraft arrives at the 180 degree position (imagine the back stretch of a racetrack), you roll the plane into a left turn so that it is aligned along the ship's track and you reestablish a straight and level attitude for the final approach. As the number two aircraft in the pattern, I was watching both the ship and the plane ahead of me as I reached the beam position (180 degree) on my initial pass. To my horror, the plane in front of me stalled and plunged into the water. It was a surreal moment and it was almost as if it did not, or could not, happen. I immediately added power, retracted my landing gear, closed my canopy, and proceeded to the holding pattern in accordance with our briefing instructions. The rescue helicopter, which was hovering in the plane guard position on the starboard side of the ship's fantail, swooped in and had the drenched student in the hoist in minutes. The aircraft was never recovered.

Act two of the drama resumed about 20 minutes later when I successfully grabbed my first arresting wire on a carrier deck. It was a very abrupt landing even though the relative velocity between ship and aircraft was only about 90 knots. Taking off from a carrier deck is quite easy with the wind down the deck assisting you in establishing flying speed. After my second or third landing, I looked around and could not see anyone else in the pattern and thought that I had missed a radio communication telling everyone to return to the beach. It turned out that the pilot behind me broke his shoulder harness upon landing and they pulled his aircraft to the hangar deck to fix the strap. My remaining landings went off without a hitch.

Here is a postscript on the pilot who stalled and plunged into the bay. He broke his nose on impact but was otherwise uninjured. An article in the local base newspaper quoted him from his hospital bed saying that he was thankful he had trained in the Dilbert Dunker and was anxious to get back in the air. A month later I noticed a two line statement in the same base paper. He had submitted a DOR (dropped at own request). I surmised that during his recuperation period he mulled over his future and had second thoughts about a flying career.

Several events occurred at Pensacola that were not directly associated with flying. The first was running into the plebe I mentored at the Academy (recall that each first year student is assigned a senior), Ed Gross. He was starting flight training just as I was finishing. He owned a red sports car, which was fairly typical for bachelor aviators, and my two-year-old son Steve fell in love with it. He used to just sit in Ed's car pretending he was driving and when Ed would drive him around the block, Steve always had a huge smile on his face. Ed completed flight training and went into A-4s (jet attack). A sad ending; he was killed in an aircraft accident about five years later, leaving a wife and small daughter Ed never really got to know.

Steve and I were sitting on our porch one Sunday in the fall of 1959 and I asked him what color was the car driving past our house?

"Blue," he correctly stated. When I inquired about the next red car, he smiled and said "red." At that point I called Donna out to observe her little genius who had mastered colors before the age of two.

"What color is that (black) car, Stephen?" I asked, knowing how impressed his mother would be.

"Blue," he replied.

"And the next (green)?"

"Red," he shouted.

Each succeeding answer was either blue or red regardless of the actual color. I realized I would have to postpone use of the word precocious until another day.

There was a couple that lived just a block from us in Pensacola. He was an ensign from the Class of 1958 (Will's class) by the name of Al Swanson. I knew of him from the Academy because he played varsity football and basketball, a real natural athlete. His wife's name was Carol and she hailed from a well-to-do family from the suburbs of Philadelphia. They were close friends of Al's classmate, John McCain, who was then a bachelor. I was surprised when I heard Al and Carol had gotten a divorce but I was shocked to find out she married John shortly thereafter. Their marriage survived the six or so years when McCain was a POW. Unfortunately, they separated shortly after his return from captivity.

Selection of which aircraft type a new pilot would get to fly was a really big deal during flight training, and choosing occurred just before one qualified on the carrier. Many candidates entered the program with their only goal being to fly jets. Others had a dream of becoming a commercial pilot and consequently preferred multi-engine patrol aircraft. A few were ambivalent and hoped to get their wings without dying in the process. The selection of helicopters as a career choice was just becoming popular in late 1959. It turned out I was initially turned down for a helicopter slot but was accepted for jet training. I quickly got over my disappointment when, several days later I was informed that my first choice, helicopter training, was granted. One other advantage of advanced training in helos was that we would not have to move from Pensacola until the spring of 1960. With Donna pregnant with our second child, avoiding a move was welcome.

Advanced training for the helicopter students consisted of four months of mastering instrument flying in a fixed wing, Beechcraft twin engine SNB. It was definitely a low performance passenger airplane that had been in the inventory for ages. After takeoff, the student pilot would wear 'blinders' or a hood to prevent him from seeing anything except the instrument panel. Flights were normally three hours long with a second student taking the controls for the last ninety minutes of the sortie. Instrument flying without automatic flight features was intense so an hour and a half under the hood was more than sufficient.

Most pilots prefer flying under visual conditions so they can see outside the cockpit. I have always felt most comfortable flying using instruments as a reference to navigate and control the plane. During these four months of advanced training in the SNB, I received the highest flight grades vis-à-vis other phases of training. (I am amused how often writers whose intent is to sound intellectual use the French term vis-à-vis incorrectly. The phrase most commonly means in comparison with.)

In December, Donna gave birth to Douglas Raymond. He had large eyes in relation to the size of his head, so identifying Doug was easy looking at family photos of the family in the early 1960s. Steve seemed to accept the addition to the family with only mild interest and he showed no signs of sibling disapproval.

Baby Douglas was the center of attention over the Christmas holidays, after driving to Northumberland, PA, Donna's hometown. The three week break was welcome even though it meant trading the warm Florida sunshine for the damp and cold Northeast.

While making the chilly drive to PA, I was reminded of a bachelor student pilot who bought a sports car right out of the Academy and, to cut down on the cost, decided to forego the purchase of a heater. Before the holidays, he offered a ride to a colleague if he would share gas costs since they were both going to New York City. The passenger was so cold by the time they arrived at their destination that he almost strangled the proud owner of the hot new sports car. The frozen passenger paid for an airline ticket to make the return trip in January. It never occurred to the sports car owner that if he couldn't afford a heater, perhaps the monthly payments on the car were too high. But, then again, maybe 'chick magnets' cannot be truly evaluated by normal financial methodology.

With 35 hours logged in the SNB, I felt like a veteran getting back into the saddle after the three week layoff. The new year (1960) would bring all sorts of adventures, including helicopter training and orders to a fleet helicopter squadron. The final 30 hours of advanced instrument flying were completed in four weeks and I started helo flying a week later. The transition from fixed wing to rotary wing aircraft was similar to being introduced to new math after a lifetime of using old math. Just as you became familiar with the rules of the house, they change most of the rules.

About the only advantage of learning to fly airplanes before you attempt helicopters is familiarity of communicating with the tower and aircraft controllers. Knowledge of aircraft flight patterns is also a plus. But the success rates of experienced airplane pilots transitioning to helicopters are only marginally higher than student pilots who begin with helicopters. The reason appears to be the fact that controls in the helicopter do not operate in a manner similar to an airplane. Consequently, an experienced fixed wing aviator has to spend some of his time unlearning established habit patterns of flying fixed wing aircraft.

The most challenging task to master in helicopter training is learning to hover. Movement of the cyclic pitch stick (the one that controls your movement over the ground) is so minute that one just has to think about changing its position. A common tendency is to overcompensate for movement over the ground and one is soon in a pilot induced oscillation (PIO). For example, the first day of hovering practice the instructor will often establish the helicopter in a stable hover in the middle of a large field and direct the student to stay within the confines of the field. Usually the student starts drifting left and immediately moves the cyclic right, which stops the left drift but the aircraft is moving right at a more rapid rate. An even more abrupt movement in the control arrests the right movement and the instructor is soon shouting, "I have control." Practice, of course, is the key and in a few hours the helicopter is correctly responding to your smaller inputs.

Student pilots learn to fly helicopters with no automatic flight aids. As you become more proficient in your flight skills, the more advanced helicopters become easier to fly because of more sophisticated flight controls as well as automatic fuel controls that maintain rotor revolutions. It all seems a little backwards, but a little humility when learning to fly might instill some needed respect for the machine that hopefully will keep you alive.

A mindset that is drilled into novice helo pilots is always to have an emergency landing site picked out and always know the wind direction and velocity. That way, you can immediately maneuver the aircraft into a safe autorotation (disconnecting the rotor blades from the engine and using the inertia of the rotor blades to land safely) if an engine fails. To this day, I observe the direction of smoke coming out of chimneys and estimate wind speed as I drive my car on the highway. The knowledge is of absolutely no value but I can't get it out of my head.

After two months and 34 hours in the two man, bubble top HTL-6 helicopter, I graduated into a heavier helo that had actually been used in the fleet in the 1950s, the HO4S built by Sikorsky. It was grossly underpowered and I was surprised that it had been used for submarine detection, which requires carrying a crew of two as well as a SONAR transducer.

After 17 instructional hops and 11 solo flights, I was certified to fly U.S. Navy helicopters and received my wings on April 20, 1960. At the wings ceremony, two Navy and three Marine Corps officers received their designation as naval aviators. We all repeated the Navy Flyer's Creed. It is:

"I am a United States Navy flyer. My countrymen built the best airplane in the world and entrusted it to me. They trained me to fly it. I will use it to the absolute limit of my power. With my fellow pilots, aircrews, and deck crews, my plane and I will do anything necessary to carry out our tremendous responsibilities. I will always remember we are part of an unbeatable combat team, the United States Navy. When the going is fast and rough, I will not falter. I will be uncompromising in every blow I strike. I will be humble in victory. I am a United States Navy flyer. I have dedicated myself to my country, with its many millions of all races, colors, and creeds. They and their way of life are worthy of my greatest protective effort. I ask the help of God in making that effort great enough."

With those words as inspiration and sporting a shiny new set of gold wings, I made preparations to move my family to the West Coast and commence a four-year assignment in Helicopter Anti-Submarine Squadron Two (HS-2), home ported in San Diego.

Because we had a short trip planned to New York City and to visit Brother Will, stationed near the city, before our cross country journey, I dropped a short note to CBS telling them I would be in NYC and could be available as a contestant on Garry Moore's "I've Got a Secret" television show. The quiz show was one of the most watched on television. A panel of four personalities (Bill Cullen, Henry Morgan, Bess Myerson and Betsy Palmer) would attempt to guess a contestant's secret that would be shared with the viewing audience. After receiving no reply, I accepted the fact that my postcard three cent investment was a failure. (I did not know that federal regulations required Department of Defense approval allowing a military member to appear on a commercial broadcast.)

CHAPTER 8

Cleared To Lift Off

It is generally inadvisable to eject directly over the area you just bombed.

THERE HAS ALWAYS been a prestige hierarchy within the Navy with aviators and submariners looking down their noses at surface ship officers. Within the black-shoe (surface ship) navy, duty on a combatant ship is considered superior to a support vessel such as a supply ship or a tanker. All naval officers with flag rank (admiral) aspirations are aware of the significance of career-enhancing billets. They often try to influence the personnel officers who assign these positions so their promotion opportunities are enhanced.

Naval aviation was no exception. Fighter pilots were in the vanguard and drivers of cargo planes brought up the rear. In between were attack, carrier-based S-2s (fixed wing prop planes) and patrol aircraft. In 1960 helicopters were not even considered in the pecking order, although helo drivers did look down on blimp pilots.

The helicopter squadrons had one of the easiest missions in the Navy since it involved no night flying and consequently attracted some of the least professional aviators in the fleet.

It was not uncommon in the 1950s for student aviators, who received excessive 'downs' (unsatisfactory flights) in fixed wing flight training to be reassigned to the helicopter pipeline rather than be washed out of the program. Rotary wing pilots did not even maintain their proficiency in flying under instrument conditions in the late 1950s and early 1960s. In fact, it was standard for helicopter pilots on cross country flights to use an Esso road map for low-level navigating rather than the published aviation charts. So few helicopter-qualified lieutenant commanders were promoted to the rank of commander and subsequently screened for command (as CO of an aircraft squadron), that aviators from other specialties, such as patrol planes, were sent to helicopter training. This policy was initiated so there would be enough commanding officers to fill the leadership vacancies in helicopter squadrons.

Lest I paint too grim a picture, let me say that there were many talented pilots in helicopter squadrons in 1960 when I reported to Helicopter Anti-Submarine Squadron Two (HS-2) for duty. It was just that the senior aviators were not the hard-charging, knowledgeable leaders that were so common in the fighter and attack squadrons.

The Wright family was pleased to receive orders to San Diego following flight training since the other options were Quonset Point, Rhode Island or Norfolk, Virginia. It was not that we disliked the East Coast but the black shoe tour in Hawaii spoiled us regarding fair weather duty stations.

The Navy expected its members to drive an average of 500 miles a day between duty stations and it was generally understood regarding the time it took to rent a house at your new home port. Seldom did junior officers purchase houses in the early 1960s since few had the necessary down payment required. Aviators were paid flight pay, which amounted to $100 a month on top of base pay plus an allowance for housing and messing. The total came to about $500 a month for a married junior lieutenant, which was a livable wage but far from living high on the hog.

For a PCS (permanent change of station) move, it was permissible to take an advance on your salary (called a dead horse) and pay it back in six equal parts over the next half-year. This allowed you sufficient funds to pay two months rent plus a damage deposit, if required. Most junior officers took advantage of this benefit even though it meant a reduced standard of living until the loan was paid back. It was clearly a case of living a life of genteel poverty if you wanted to serve in the military services in the 1950s and 1960s.

After a quick visit to realtors south of San Diego, we rented a modest three-bedroom house on Shasta Street in Chula Vista, about eight miles from Ream Field, the helicopter base in Imperial Beach, California. HS-2 had departed its homeport on board the USS *Hornet*, an ASW carrier used for hunting and destroying enemy submarines. I bid a fond adieu to Donna and the two boys and flew off to Honolulu to join the squadron for a six-month deployment in the Western Pacific. Being a Navy wife was not the easiest existence in the universe.

There was something special about one's first squadron. Almost instant camaraderie existed among the junior officers and the atmosphere in the ready room was a combination of wonderment, exhilaration and joie de vivre (joy of living). It may have been the common danger, the unusual profession of flying helicopters for a living or the enjoyment that comes from hanging around iconoclastic people who have chosen to serve their country. Everyone seemed to view life in an optimistic manner and the only restrictions to success were self-imposed. And, there were always a lot of laughs. Any acts of pretension were quickly challenged and dealt with in an appropriate (sarcastic) manner.

Hoppy Hohenstein, my roommate at the Academy, was stationed on a submarine home ported in Hawaii so I called him right after reporting for duty on the *Hornet*. He was going to sea for a couple of weeks but loaned me his new convertible to use while he was out of town. I sub-loaned his car to a friend and squadron mate, Ted Sholl, whose wife, Marion, had flown over for a short vacation before the extended cruise to West Pac. I got the car back in good shape but took it on a short trip around the island and dented the fender on some protrusion from the underbrush. I had to sweet talk a body shop man to repair and touch up the damaged part before Hoppy returned. I think the lesson to be learned from this incident was that Tabor values (what's mine is yours) are not always valid in the real world. It would have been hard to explain to Hoppy why I loaned his car to a friend when the gift wasn't mine to give.

All ASW helicopter squadrons were flying the Sikorsky HSS-1, later designated the SH-34, when the Department of Defense created common designator codes for all U.S. aircraft. The 'Hiss one' was a single engine, dual-pilot, single-lifting-rotor helicopter with two crewmen that operated the SONAR. Their primary mission was detecting enemy submarines. A secondary mission was rescuing downed airmen or picking up unfortunate souls that fell overboard.

Incidentally, trying to locate a person in the ocean is difficult since the eye is most effective in detecting objects that are moving. But with mile upon square mile of rough water, there is a low probability of picking up a bobbing helmet or head. Pilots carry green dye in their flight suits, which is quite effective when activated since that can be seen many miles away. They also carry shark repellant but it is doubtful that it is effective in discouraging sharks. However, the psychological lift that it gives the user is worth the cost of a little duplicity on the part of the Navy.

All military helicopters were underpowered and the HSS-1 was no exception. On certain days when the temperature was warm and winds were low, there was insufficient power generated to maintain a hover. On those days, the procedure was to burn down several hundred pounds of fuel until the weight was reduced to an acceptable level. The key was to develop the skill to attempt a hover but not commit until you were sure there was sufficient power to maintain it. Pilots were given a heads-up during the briefing when environmental conditions were marginal. I don't know of a single case of an aircraft that was lost because of insufficient power available going into a hover. I do know of one case in HS-2 of a pilot who lost his Nr tachometer (the indicator that shows how many rpm the main rotor is turning) in a hover and lowered his collective (controls the pitch of the main rotor blades, equivalent to a throttle in a fixed wing aircraft), settling into the water. Since there were no floatation devices on the helicopter, it immediately sank. The official accident report listed sudden engine failure, causing loss of rotor rpm as the primary cause. No one on board the aircraft remembered a quiet environment (no engine noise) as the aircraft settled into the water. Other than getting soaked, the aircrew was uninjured.

My first aviation cruise to the Pacific was exciting since it involved a fair amount of flying (an average of 24 flight hours per month) including sightseeing flights in the Philippines and Japan. And I also volunteered to stand bridge watches to qualify as officer-of-the-deck (OOD) on a carrier. These watches were all during night operations since the helicopters didn't fly at night while underway. I found expectations of an OOD on a carrier much lower than those on a destroyer. I sensed the captain was uneasy letting an Airedale from a helo squadron stand the top watch so after just a few watches as OOD, I asked the navigator to let others have the opportunity since it was not benefiting me in any way. I did get my qualification recorded in my file, which was my primary purpose all along.

It was not a sound squadron policy to allow rotary wing pilots to fly in foreign countries without specific and useful missions, such as checking out new pilots and maintaining proficiency in the aircraft. Some pilots, however, flew at unauthorized low altitudes (flathatting), chased water buffalo in the Philippines off cliffs or hovered over the great Buddha at Nara, Japan, and touched one wheel on his head. Incidents such as these were never reported to authorities and the pilots simply had amusing stories to tell at happy hour.

During this cruise, it was determined that a fleet introduction program (FIP) would be conducted to train personnel in the newly designed HSS-2, a Sikorsky night ASW helicopter equipped with advanced SONAR and jet turbine engines. A team of pilots and maintenance men was to be selected from each coast shortly after our deployment and would spend several months of training at Key West Naval Air Station in Florida under the tutelage of Sikorsky production pilots. I was one of twenty of the thirty pilots that came from fleet squadrons. The remainder of the pilots would be supplied from the replacement air groups (RAG), squadrons charged with training newly assigned fleet pilots in the SH-3A helicopter. Few of the FIP pilots selected realized the immensity of the task ahead. Within the year, we would be deploying with sixteen night-flying helicopters and carrying out a mission that, unlike our previous mission, one of the easiest in aviation, was one that was arguably one of the most challenging. To some, it was an opportunity to visit Key West for three months, and to add 50 flight hours in a new helicopter to their logbook.

We returned from cruise one week before Christmas in 1960. Squadrons would normally fly off when the carrier was one day from port, about 200 miles. Pilots were selected to fly based on seniority, but if your helicopter went down on deck with a maintenance problem, you did not have the authority to bump more junior officers flying in another aircraft and take their place. It was remarkable there were not more accidents during fly-offs since nearly every pilot was stricken with get-home-itis. I remember Max Quitiquit taking a helo that had its main rotor blades about one foot out of track (each of the five main rotor blades should follow one another in the same horizontal plane). The crew must have had its teeth shaken loose because of the low frequency vibration by the time they landed at home base.

Following the Christmas holidays, HS-2 resumed its normal training schedule, consisting of ASW flights, hops in the ground simulator practicing emergencies and other flight procedures as well as studying the procedures in the standardization (NATOPS) manual. It was also time for extracurricular sports.

That winter HS-2 won the intramural basketball title, consisting of all squadrons based at Ream Field, by defeating HS-4 in the title game, 35 to 29. We came back from a one-point deficit at halftime to capture the championship and I was fortunate enough to be picked on the tournament all-star team. Our team played a 30 game schedule and went undefeated.

The FIP pilots selected from HS-2 were: Lcdr. Roy Winslett, two Lieutenants, Ted Sholl and me, and seven Lieutenant (junior grade) officers, Bruce Borquist, Tom Bartholomew, Roger Edson, Gus Gustaveson, Paul Bateman, Carl Stokes and Wally Weller. All were capable aviators and a few were excellent. All team members were responsible for absorbing the tricks of the trade from factory pilots and creating a squadron-wide training program that would not only be effective in chasing enemy submarines but would keep aircrews alive for the next several years. I chose to go unaccompanied for the three-month assignment, both for financial reasons as well as the fact that Donna was expecting another addition to the family.

Key West is an interesting city 100 miles southwest of Miami. Before 1938, the only way to visit the place was by water, air, or railroad. It should surprise no one that the inhabitants were a tad provincial. Its population of 32,000 people had doubled from 1940 to 1961 and the city was best known as the residence of author Ernest Hemingway and the winter White House of Harry Truman in the late 1940s. The U.S. Navy had a presence in Key West for years and the weather was ideal for flying all year round.

The flight program for the HSS-2 ran smoothly with each pilot averaging twenty hours a month for the months of June, July and August. One can only imagine how hot it is in the summer at Key West, which is 24.5 degrees North latitude. There were no air conditioners in the new helicopters although 100 percent of the pilots would have voted for their inclusion as mission-essential equipment. The temperature in the cockpit often reached 120 degrees F when the aircraft were parked in the sun for an afternoon launch. The protective flight suit and gloves added to our misery.

In addition to flying and learning about the helicopter's systems, I also volunteered to umpire Little League baseball games. I was paid for the effort so it was not entirely an altruistic endeavor. It was my first experience dealing with Little League parents. The most ignorant were among the loudest critics. The kids were great, which made my efforts worthwhile. Our car was left in San Diego with Donna and the two boys so I purchased a bicycle to pedal around the town and to ball games.

Life in the bachelor officer's quarters was quite acceptable and living expenses were really low so an unaccompanied 90-day temporary assignment seemed normal. A few pilots, who were married but childless, brought their wives to Key West at their own expense and felt it was money well spent.

In September, the new HS-2 Commanding Officer, Owen R. Toon, flew commercially to Key West to ferry one of the four or five helicopters used in the fleet introduction program, cross-country to San Diego. We logged 25 hours in the air on the 2,000-mile trip and having the skipper as a co-pilot (who smoked cigars for four straight days), I considered above and beyond the call of duty.

The following month Donna gave birth to our third son, John Charles. This was supposed to be a daughter and the end of child-bearing in the Wright household. Both Steve and Doug seemed reasonably pleased to have another sibling in the family. Three children under the age of five, including an infant, cannot be what Donna had in mind when she signed up for the glamorous life as the wife of a naval aviator.

With only eight months to get the entire squadron checked out in the new helicopter, the winter and spring were rather hectic in HS-2 but there was an unprecedented air of enthusiasm within the group since we had been chosen, not only to support fleet introduction, but also to take the HSS-2 on its first deployment to West Pac. Cockpit layout pictures were posted in the bathroom stalls (heads) so there would be no time wasted during even private moments.

In our enthusiasm to make the new helicopter successful in fleet operations, we occasionally took risks that, in retrospect, were foolish. HS-2 was on call to pursue any unidentified submarine contacts that were generated from our fixed-sensors system that was deployed off the West Coast. One evening I received a request to proceed 100 miles due west of San Diego and investigate an unknown contact. As I launched from Ream Field into the dark night with a co-pilot that was so inexperienced that I had to direct him which buttons to activate, my 'playmate' (second helicopter in the flight) reported a problem with his mission avionics and aborted the flight.

I was now on my own in a single-helicopter sortie to investigate a contact 100 miles off the coast with no means of being rescued in the event our aircraft ended up in the water. We pressed on to datum (target's last known position) and searched for an hour or so without success. After returning to base, I concluded I had made an emotional rather than an intellectual decision to prosecute a questionable contact in conditions that put the lives of my entire crew at risk. Too much boldness in aviation can shorten one's lifespan considerably.

On May 2, 1962, sixteen HSS-2 helicopters flew aboard the USS Hornet in San Diego and proceeded to Hawaii for several weeks of submarine operations before making the final push across the Pacific Ocean to operate out of Naval Station Subic Bay in the Philippine Islands.

As soon as we docked in Pearl Harbor, I received a telephone call from Irma Reichert of CBS. She had cleared it with the Defense Department in Washington for Will and me to appear on Garry Moore's "I've Got a Secret" to air on Monday May 14th. She said a telegram would follow giving all the details. Will was stationed at Stewart Air Force Base in upstate New York so he had only a two-hour car ride to get to the city but I had to fly 5,000 miles to Idlewild Airport. Apparently we were selected based on the postcard I had sent in early 1960, and because Armed Forces Day coincided with the May show.

The whole adventure was interesting because we got to see a television production from the inside as a contestant. CBS prepaid my airline ticket and directed me to take the limousine bus to NYC and then take the airline terminal taxi to the Hotel Victoria where a double room was reserved for us. The only unusual event that occurred was a short conversation I had with a woman passenger on the bus. When she found out I was in the Navy, she asked why I was not in uniform. It puzzled me at the time but later I remembered that it was a federal law during the war years for all military personnel to wear their uniforms at all times.

We were directed to call CBS Monday morning at 10:45 for further directions. As it turned out, the hotel was right around the corner from the studio so we walked over and met the production staff about noon. They had a deli lunch delivered to the set and told us to help ourselves. About two p.m. the walk-through started. This was done with stand-in personnel for timing purposes. Garry Moore participated and was cordial to both Will and me.

During rehearsal when I heard the plan to introduce Will by name, I commented to Garry that the panel would have no problem with the secret. He replied that the purpose of the show was entertainment, not to stump the panel. With that information, I immediately told him we would like to donate any money that we won to the Damon Runyon Cancer Fund. With 40 dollars awarded for each wrong answer, I was fairly sure the contest would be over quickly and a donation from armed forces personnel would be a nice public relations touch.

Here is the news article from the *Doylestown Intelligencer* the following day:

Two brothers, who formerly lived at the Tabor Home near Doylestown, and are Central Bucks High School graduates, as well as graduates of the U.S. Naval Academy at Annapolis, Maryland, appeared on "I've Got A Secret" last night.

Lt. Wilbur Wright, who is now stationed with the Air Force at a base at Newburgh, New York, appeared on the television panel show and whispered to the emcee, Garry Moore, that his secret was that his brother, Orville Wright, was backstage in the television studio.

Miss Betsy Palmer, stage and screen actress and one of the panelists, began the questioning. She broke the ice when she asked, "Is your secret two legged?"

The next panelist, Henry Morgan, asked, "Is Orville Wright backstage?"

"Yes," said Wilbur and the two brothers' television secret was over. Both brothers informed Moore they wished the $80 to be given to charity. Lt. Orville Wright, the older brother, said he is stationed at a naval air station at San Diego. Orville looked stalwart, tall, and poised while Wilbur was boyishly handsome and less formal.

Orville said his father, who was born in 1903, was named after the original Orville Wright because of his flying fame in that era.

"I would have made the mistake of my life if I hadn't gone into the Air Force," said Wilbur.

"You surely would have taken a lot if kidding if you had become a Marine," said Moore.

The two brothers looked handsome, trim and had engaging personalities on television.

Unfortunately, there was no advance publicity about their telecast appearance and many Central Bucks television viewers, who went to school with them, played sports and knew them from boyhood through high school, missed their debut.

Following the taping of the show, Will and I were invited by Garry Moore and the production staff to a small restaurant in the vicinity of the CBS studio to have dinner and watch the show as it aired. It was great fun and especially nice to see my brother again. The producers gave us each $25 a day spending money plus paid all our expenses. They offered to pick up the tab if we wanted to extend our vacation in the city but we declined and headed back to our respective bases.

After returning to the *Hornet*, I found out the show was opposite Bob Hope and several officers in the wardroom strongly objected to switching that off to see "I've Got a Secret." There was almost a brawl on the ship but they finally agreed to change the channel and watch Garry Moore. (Garry died in 1993 at age 78.)

Deploying with a new model aircraft is always interesting because the airframes, engines and mission equipment are immature and periodic inspections are necessary to judge how much longer the components can be flown before they are replaced. For instance, the General Electric T-58 engine was designed to be changed after 1,000 flight hours but when HS-2 deployed in mid-1962, the engine life was established at 200 hours. These high-time engines were sent back to the factory for inspection of excessive wear. Incrementally, the life of the engines would be extended until the design limit plus a safety margin was reached. In 1962, the engines were clearly not ready for fleet deployment. There was always visible hydraulic fluid or engine oil during pre-flight inspections. If the leaks were just oozing, we would accept the helicopter for flight. During the cruise, over 100 T-58 engines were replaced with only two attaining high time of 200 hours.

The HSS-2 helicopter weighed in at 20,000 pounds and could hover on one of its two engines if the winds were blowing at a speed of 20 knots (a knot is one nautical mile per hour or about 1/8 faster than a mile per hour) or more. It did have an amphibious-shaped hull so the airframe would float in low sea states (height of waves under two feet). It had a top speed of 150 knots (170 mph) and could climb to about 15,000 feet altitude. Its basic autopilot would allow hands-off flight and the aircraft would transition automatically from forward flight into a hover for night dipping of the SONAR. The transition equipment was reasonably reliable but required constant monitoring by the pilots because a malfunction at such low altitudes could be disastrous.

The primary mission of the helicopter was to search, track and drop weapons on enemy submarines. Helos worked in concert with destroyers and fixed wing S-2 aircraft. When rotary and fixed wing aircraft were operating in the same airspace, a 200-foot floor was specified for fixed wing planes and a 150-foot ceiling for the helicopters. So the helo world existed between 150-foot base (top) altitude and 40 feet, which was the hovering height when the SONAR was lowered. At night, the mission was accomplished by flying solely on instruments with the pilots only looking out of the cockpit to avoid collisions. A special instrument in the cockpit would inform the pilots where the SONAR cable (connection between the SONAR and the electronics in the cabin) was located in relation to the aircraft after a stable hover was established and the SONAR dome deployed. With no visible horizon or on moonless nights, it was virtually impossible to detect the actual movement of a hovering helicopter without reference to gauges.

Shortly after the deployment began, the CO decided to form night-pilot teams that consisted of putting two aircraft commanders in each helicopter that flew after sunset. The less experienced pilots were relegated to daylight flying. This concept was sound from a safety-of-flight standpoint but did not conform to the established procedures that called for more experienced pilots to act as mentors and trainers to the greenhorns. HS-2 ended the cruise with the same number of helicopters that flew aboard *Hornet* six months before.

An event that occurred overseas taught me a lesson. At evening meal on board the *Hornet*, I was chiding Dick Adams, a fellow pilot, about being overweight. He asked whether I would like to bet a case of beer on a footrace. Not realizing that Dick had been a sprinter in college, I quickly agreed to the challenge, confident I could easily beat him in a 100-yard race. Fortunately, another pilot, Phil Wolfe, overheard the bet and asked if anyone could get into the wager. We welcomed Phil into the contest.

The next day there were a number of interested bystanders to view the event. When the gun sounded, Dick moved out of the blocks so quickly it appeared I had failed to hear the starting pistol. I finished at least 10 yards behind Dick and Phil lumbered in a distant third. I didn't have to buy the beer but I did learn something valuable. Find out about a person's skill levels before accepting a challenge. The consequences may be more severe than a meal of humble pie.

In October 1962, the Department of Defense put out a directive that gave military aircraft a common designator across all services. The HSS-2 was renamed as the SH-3A with the S standing for anti-submarine. By Christmas, the second deployments of the SH-3A had begun to West Pac by HS-6 and to the Med by HS-9. The trouble was that both these squadrons had lost several helicopters while conducting night operations. This trend continued with both organizations averaging one fatal accident every 90 days. In short order, the pilots were blaming the radar altimeter (the device which indicates true altitude over the water). It was soon evident that a low-altitude warning device would have to be installed to alert the pilots that the aircraft was below the desired altitude and about to hit the water. That improvement to the radar altimeter took about a year to design, test and install in all fleet aircraft. Meanwhile, the fatalities continued at unprecedented rates. The final tally of fatal accidents in an 18-month period was 12, divided equally between HS-6 and HS-9. Some of the squadron's best pilots were involved and it had a chilling effect on the morale of all squadron aircrews during that time frame. Neither squadron decided to fly with the night-team concept.

A side note about accidents and death in the military. The general public believes the military favors war and combat. If one thinks about who makes the sacrifice and who takes the risks during combat, the conclusion about military and war is obviously flawed. Members of the armed services, with few exceptions, do not like war and they hate to be shot at.

Aircraft accidents occur. Every military pilot or air crewman I have ever associated with accepts that fact. Because of it, insensitivity builds up within the minds of military pilots concerning death. The vast majority of fatal accidents are caused by pilot error. A much smaller percentage is caused by equipment failure and weather is responsible for a few accidents. As sad as attending a memorial service or funeral of a shipmate is, there is a pervasive attitude within the ranks of aviators that creates a certain emotional detachment from the deceased. It is not that you don't care about the well-being of the widow or her family that is now without a breadwinner, it is just a fact that is accepted as the price that might have to be paid by anyone in the world of military flight.

A normal tour of sea duty for an aviator was three to four years. The Bureau of Personnel (BuPers) has varied this time-frame over the years but they found a four-year tour was detrimental to morale and family cohesion. After observing numerous parties for departing pilots, I felt the squadron should do more than give the departing officer a plaque and a firm handshake. I created an HS-2 Commendation, which was a scroll of eight or nine paragraphs of what the pilot had accomplished while in the squadron. It had the official seal at the top and the recipient's name, rank and serial number in Leroy lettering. After an initial paragraph documenting the number of total and night flight hours, the subsequent paragraphs highlighted every embarrassing mistake made by the recipient during his time in the squadron. It was typed on parchment paper and presented as a scroll.

The first pilot who received the bogus commendation had it framed and hung it in his den. I modified subsequent awards by framing them before presentation. I felt that, at the very least, we should give a personalized gift to show our appreciation for their efforts in the past three or four years.

Only once did a departing officer leave his award behind. There were references in Gordon Ziegler's commendation about spending 8,000 yen on drinks for a bar girl in Sasebo, Japan, and then being stood up by her after closing time. He knew his wife would not see the humor in the incident.

By the time my third deployment in HS-2 rolled around in October of 1963, most of the FIP-trained pilots had moved on to greener pastures. Charley Jones had taken over from Owen Toon as CO and his XO was a fairly controversial Commander, Dewey Wade. I was rooming with John Higginson, an officer who was actually drafted into the Navy as an enlisted man. We had been friends since he joined the squadron about six months after I did and our families socialized on many occasions. John was the quintessential unflappable man, which is quite advantageous. He subsequently was one of the first helicopter admirals in the Navy.

With my background as a surface ship SONAR officer and my experience in the SH-3A helicopter, I was in the forefront of developing tactics to prosecute enemy submarines. I represented HS-2 on the Air Group ASW Tactics Board. When the Officer-in-Charge (OIC) of the Airborne Early Warning Detachment, Lt. Nelson, reported on board the Hornet, he was surprised to find out that I ignored him. He was the same arrogant flight instructor from Saufley Field who gave me a 'down' to show me who was the boss in the cockpit.

He initially seemed mildly amused that I would look right through him as if he did not exist. But after several weeks it started to bother him. He pulled my roommate, John Higginson, aside one day and asked him why I was trying to humiliate him. John reminded him of his rank-pulling stunt in primary training. Lt. Nelson responded, "How was I to know he was somebody?"

The sad conclusion of this incident occurred about a month later during night flight operations. On a landing attempt, Lt. Nelson's tail hook separated from his aircraft. He was now airborne with no means of getting aboard. A barrier made of webbing could be rigged across the deck but that would take some time and his aircraft was running low on fuel. Neither the pilot nor the landing signal officer (LSO) was aware that the aircraft had no restraining hook. On the next pass, the LSO waved Lt. Nelson off because of improper line-up but the pilot chose to override the wave-off and landed in a skid. His A-1 Skyraider slammed into the pack of aircraft parked aft of the carrier's superstructure and burst into flames. Lt. Nelson did not survive the crash. An incident like this gives one pause to question the wisdom of turning anyone into a non-person for personal reasons. Although intellectually I knew I did not possess any extraordinary power, I decided to eliminate that curse from my arsenal.

My fifth West Pac cruise in six years of commissioned service was different from the other four. It was my first Christmas away from home. I wrote a family Christmas letter and had it duplicated at a local Japanese printing company. Here are a few excerpts from the epistle:

"The first half-year was spent in the normal harried manner of our family with basketball games, little theater plays, new restaurants, kindergarten crises and a three-week aircraft maintenance school for Orv in San Francisco. His departure coincided with the first case of measles, which spread throughout the family, followed closely by mumps. A very trying three weeks at 415 Shasta Street.

Steve passed a milestone in his life in September when he started first grade. He remains unimpressed, having had a year of preparation in the same school. Like most children, he isn't working up to his potential, but he is showing unusual creative ability and we're confident he can make it. Doug remains indifferent regarding Steve's academic achievements and delights in teasing him about the occasional 'poor' scrawled across his schoolwork.

Doug attends nursery school twice a week and is a sure bet to be teacher's pet when he starts school. John, alone, remains uneducated. He is, however, a hard worker around the house and in the yard. There is still a need in this country for the honest, hardworking and uneducated individuals. So we haven't given up on John, age two, yet."

The cruise was uneventful. We spent most of our time operating out of Japanese ports rather than the Philippine ports. The Commanding Officer did experience a gear-up landing during a shore-based flight the morning after a squadron party. The damage was minimal and was repaired by the local maintenance depot at Iwakuni, Japan. As far as I know, there was no record of the incident submitted. An electronic device was subsequently installed in the cockpit to warn pilots if their landing gear was still up when their altitude was below 50 feet. No instrument was installed to detect pilots with hangovers.

During our port visit to Hong Kong, three or four officers in the squadron were scheduled to transfer. I volunteered to make arrangements for their going-away party. The minute I left the carrier, I ran into a friend who was ship's company on the Hornet on my first cruise. He was living in Hong Kong and running a business selling bonded liquor. I relayed my need to arrange a suitable departure party for some shipmates and he offered to help. I met him for dinner that evening and he volunteered his large flat along with booze at rock-bottom prices. He also hired a local three-piece band and invited all the young English-speaking lady friends who he knew in the Colony to the party. The total cost of this affair came to five dollars per head. It was a huge success and everyone had a marvelous time. In looking back on four years in HS-2, I received the most compliments by being the architect of this party in Hong Kong. Sometimes in life, luck is as important as skill and cunning.

With my four-year tour in HS-2 concluding in May 1964, I evaluated the options open to me. An advanced degree at the Navy's Post Graduate School in Monterey, California, would be beneficial but a more interesting choice might be the Test Pilot School (TPS) at Patuxent (Pax) River, Maryland. The latter seemed to be more prestigious and the recent addition of a specific rotary wing course could give a young helicopter pilot a leg-up when it came to promotion for captain or flag rank. With that as my criterion, I applied to the Navy Test Pilot School. My CO, Dewey Wade, gave me a glowing endorsement.

Before the cruise ended in April, I had two sets of orders in hand. One was for Post Graduate School to study oceanography and the other was for Test Pilot School at Pax River. I just sat tight and let BuPers sort it out. I was not going to tempt fate and push for one or the other.

My last flight in HS-2 was on the first of May in 1964. By then I had flown almost 1,300 hours in helicopters and was just short of 1,000 hours in the SH-3. At my departure party I received a framed commendation award. The orders to PG school were cancelled so the Wrights set off to St. Mary's County in Maryland for the next three years.

CHAPTER **9**

Testing Helicopters and Other Adventures

Logic is a systematic method of coming to the wrong conclusion with confidence.

DURING THE KENNEDY administration it was determined that members of the armed services were getting flabby and the government should solve that problem by setting appropriate standards of fitness for all personnel in the military. A set of aerobic and strength exercises was established with equivalent scores. These tests were to be conducted annually and the results determined whether the warrior continued to serve at the "pleasure of the president." In other words, if you failed to pass the minimum required number of pull-ups or push-ups, your services were no longer needed. My brother's first question was, "What is the minimum, because anything in excess is wasted effort?" I always viewed it as, "What is the maximum, because you get no credit if you exceed that?" I relay this basic difference in philosophy so the reader has a better understanding of how I ended up as a naval test pilot.

My ability to fly an aircraft was probably above average but I was never a top one percentile aviator in basic piloting skills. I excelled flying under instrument conditions and I never experienced a time when I was exposed to real fear in the cockpit. By real fear, I mean when the possibility of crashing or dying was imminent. Crashing is not a term that aviators use. They are much more likely to use more precise terms such as 'hard landing, or uncontrolled water contact, or inadvertent touchdown.' To me, flying was neither exhilarating nor risky. I liked to fly and was proud to be a naval aviator, but ultimately it was a means to carry out a mission. Of course, I was interested in becoming as skilled as possible, but aviation was not something I dreamed about as a child. I applied to the U.S. Navy Test Pilot School (TPS) because it was a potential pathway to success in a very competitive environment. The risks seemed minimal and there was a certain aura of glamour among test pilots. It was also a stepping stone to my long range goal of becoming CNO. That was the background of my decision to become a naval test pilot.

Getting settled in Lexington Park was straightforward. We purchased a new house from a helicopter pilot who was awaiting orders after flunking out of TPS. He had spent a lot of time building his dream house on Blackistone Court in a nice development called Town Creek, three miles north of the air station. It was on a wooded one acre lot about a block from the main drag. With only two houses completed on the cul de sac, it was almost like living in the wilderness. The wall-to-wall carpeting in most of the house seemed to reduce the noise level generated by three young boys. They seemed to think living in their own house was a big adventure.

There was clearly a mystique about TPS in the 1960s. The astronaut program was in its infancy with Alan Shepard and John Glenn completing manned space flights in 1961 and 1962, respectively. Both were TPS graduates. Being an alumnus of the school was a Navy requirement for acceptance into the astronaut corps. I wasn't eligible on two counts; there was a six foot maximum height restriction (I was two inches too tall) and only fighter pilots were accepted, but there was enormous prestige associated with rubbing shoulders with these acknowledged heroes during TPS reunions.

The Naval Air Test Center (NATC) was at the Patuxent River Naval

Air Station in Lexington Park, Maryland, about an hour south of Washington D.C. It's mission was to evaluate both newly acquired aircraft and equipment to determine if they met the required specifications under which they were purchased, and to see if they were suitable for the Navy. The goal of TPS was to train pilots and engineers to test for detailed specifications and service suitability.

Permitting helicopter pilots to attend TPS was a fairly recent development in the Navy. There were only about six rotary wing graduates before my class. We did have a helo graduate, Don Beck, on the teaching staff at the school, and there were a few more stationed at the test center evaluating new helicopters or their weapon systems.

TPS Class 39 consisted of 14 pilots and four non pilots. The helicopter pilots reported in June 1964 to undergo a month long fixed wing familiarization as well as a jet transition course that used the T-1 jet trainer. This was really a big deal for pilots whose experience in fixed wing airplanes was limited to T-34 and T-28 trainers and twin-engine SNBs that had been in service about forty years. The helo pilots were Flight Lieutenant Ernie Booth from the Canadian Air Force, Captain Tom West, USA, Frank Tefft from Sikorsky Aircraft Company, and me.

We all seemed to adjust to the world of jets without too many sleepless nights. My biggest problem was mentally staying ahead of an aircraft that climbed 6,000 feet a minute, which was three times faster than I had been accustomed to. At 370 knots (420 mph), the T-1 moved a whole lot quicker than the 150 knots maximum speed my helicopter had attained. Another surprise was the sense of security that an ejection seat gave me. Since my operational aviation career consisted of flying at less than 1,000 feet altitude 95 percent of the time, I seldom wore a parachute. Now if an emergency arose that required bailing out, pulling the ejection curtain over your face would solve the problem immediately.

The Navy had a high accident rate in the decade of the 1950s so a program to standardize pilots had been implemented in the fleet in the early 1960s. Acceptance of the standardization program (called

NATOPS) did not come easily at the test center. Despite being a hard requirement dictated by the Chief of Naval Operations, all directors at NATC chose to ignore the guidance and continued operating as before. They felt the program was not needed. The accident rate at the test center was the highest in the fleet and it was not because of just risky-type flying. Accidents were often caused because of unfamiliarity with the systems or the aircraft that malfunctioned. It was a common saying among test pilots that, "If you show me how to start it, I can fly it."

Tom West was on a scheduled TPS dual pilot flight with Frank Tefft (Sikorsky helicopter pilot) in a T-28 fixed wing aircraft. After landing on the numbers, the tower asked him to expedite his taxi since there was an aircraft on final approach. Since he had landed on an 11,000-foot runway (and being an Army helicopter pilot) he decided to clear the landing area by taking off and flying to the far end of the runway. After landing, his brakes malfunctioned and he ended up in the boondocks with his propeller damaged. Tom was sure the incident would not only wash him out of TPS, but also cause him to lose his wings. While sitting in the cockpit awaiting the cherry picker, he asked Frank if there were any openings at Sikorsky Aircraft. The school replaced the prop that evening and the aircraft flew the following day. Other than some good-natured ribbing, no one at test pilot school thought running off the runway was serious.

I cite this attitude (similar to a fender bender where no one is hurt), so prevalent among test pilots, to highlight an event that occurred to me shortly after reporting for duty at the school. Since I had been qualified in the SH-34 helicopter, I was designated a checkout pilot for the other helo students in my class. Ernie Booth was first in line. I inquired whether he was familiar with the characteristics of the helicopter. He assured me he was and took control of the aircraft after the chocks were removed from the wheels and taxied to the takeoff area. With my guard down, Ernie immediately pulled the collective (the lever that controls the pitch of the blades increasing lift) up too rapidly, over torquing the main transmission. Realizing his error, he lowered the collective just as fast, causing the main rotor blades to exceed their RPM limits. As aircraft commander, I wasn't even airborne yet and had two major discrepancies that grounded the helicopter for a maintenance inspection and possible replacement of major components. The hard lesson I learned was to be far more skeptical when accepting another pilot's self evaluation of his capabilities.

After an initial month of 'fun flying' for the helo pilots, the remaining fixed wing aviators of Class 39 reported for duty, and the serious side of learning to be a test pilot began. Our class leader was Lieutenant Commander (Lcdr.) Ted Mead and there was a second Lcdr., Ray Ways. Four Navy Lieutenants (Harry Blackburn, Bob Dewey, George Myers and Ed O'Neal), two Marine Captains (Joe Burke and Bill Ross), one Air Force Captain (Larry Otto) and one Army Captain (Al Darling) completed the flying roster. In addition, four non aviators took the academic portion of the class. Two civil servants from NATC (Herm Kolwey and Dale Hutchins), one civilian from industry (Paul Roitsch) and one Royal Canadian Flying Officer, John Laye.

The contracting and testing side of naval aviation is markedly different from the operational side. Fleet pilots are assigned to squadrons to fly aircraft designed to accomplish missions. There is a standard format for conducting flight operations as well as recommended procedures to cope with emergencies. Mastering modern aircraft with sophisticated avionics equipment is not an easy task and innovative approaches to mission completion are not encouraged. Don't misconstrue my comment as criticism. It is a prudent system that discourages each individual pilot from experimenting with multimillion dollar weapons systems.

Testing aircraft or weapons systems to determine if they meet contractual specifications was a whole new world to a four year fleet helicopter pilot. The jargon was unfamiliar, the method of determining compliance was involved, and it often required subjective decision making when evaluating a test result. The aircraft or equipment not only had to pass specific military specifications, which were usually quantifiable, but it also had to be deemed service suitable in the eyes of the evaluator. A grading system was created to evaluate service suitability rather than using non standard descriptive adjectives.

A typical day at TPS consisted of formal classroom training in the morning and a test flight in the afternoon to put the knowledge to practical use. A written test report was required on each flight and was usually due in seven working days. Time management was of the utmost importance since there were only 24 hours in each day, and the school administrators felt no remorse in giving assignments that required the full 24 to complete. I would generally come home from school about five p.m., take a nap for an hour or so before eating dinner, and then study until midnight or one a.m. Being married with children, I studied independently, which was not the most efficient way to clear the hurdles that were thrust in our way. Most of the class joined little study groups that studied at the school and were quite effective. We did not work Sundays, but since nobody was ever caught up with flight reports, it was not a day of rest. This regimen continued for eight months.

I had always suspected that Army and Air Force pilots were not like Navy pilots. But my suspicions were never confirmed until I closely observed them at TPS. They had an irrational fear of flying over water, probably caused by none of their missions being flown over water. They would fly 20 miles out of their way to avoid the wet stuff. To naval aviators, there was always something reassuring in flying over the ocean. You knew there were not going to be any trees or wire cables to end your flight prematurely. It was also a great deal easier to put a helicopter down in the water than in a jungle or in mountainous terrain. None of that logic swayed the landlubbers. They felt at home flying under telephone wires but if a lake appeared in their path, they chose the long way round.

Although social life was practically nonexistent during the dog days of test pilot training, I recall at least one visit from Judy Yerkes, a friend from Doylestown who was married to Skip Yerkes (USNA class of 1959). We knew them quite well since, shortly after they got married, they stayed with us in San Diego for a week until they had arranged for housing. Skip was on a seven month deployment in 1965 so Judy decided to drive down to Maryland and spend a week with us. The day she arrived, I had just jumped into bed for my daily nap. Donna suggested to Judy that she just pop her head into my room and say hi. "Oh no!" she replied. "I know as soon as I go into his room, he will throw off his covers just to embarrass me." I had no idea why she had concluded that I would perform such an outrageous act, but she refused to take such a risk.

In February 1965, Class 39 graduated from Test Pilot School. The class then took a cross country trip to various aerospace companies to complement our education regarding contractors. At that time there was a 'cozy' relationship between the military services and defense contractors. At each location we were wined and dined and given rental cars to see the local sights. In Dallas, while visiting defense contractor LingTemcoVought (LTV), I was driving back to the plant with three other class members when I was rear-ended at a red light by a drunken driver who attempted to extricate herself after her bumper had locked with mine, and drive off. She failed, being arrested by the police. The only concern at LTV was how fast they could replace the broken car. It wasn't until years later that aerospace companies would be referred to as LCC's (Lying, Cheating Contractors). In the 60s they were considered loving, concerned contractors.

Class 39 started its professional life doing real testing of aircraft and avionics systems. The first order of business on any new assignment was learning the ropes from the more experienced personnel who occupied the office. I was assigned to the Weapons Systems Test (WST) Division at the Naval Air Test Center. My civilian counterpart was Archie Sherbert, a GS-12 engineer, with about 15 years' experience in avionics development work. Our primary project was to develop a Helicopter Attack System (HATS) using a single helicopter to deploy active sonobuoys and track and attack high speed submarines. For a new test pilot with a background in both surface ship and helicopter anti-submarine warfare, it was a perfect match. I loved going to work each morning to devise ways to combat the speed and stealth of the modern Russian submarines. Our early development work paid off because we were able to convince our Naval Air Systems Command (NavAir) sponsors that the concept was indeed feasible and it was prudent to design a helicopter that could track and destroy nuclear-powered submarines. The eventual product was the Light Airborne Multi-Purpose System (LAMPS) helicopter that would revolutionize anti-submarine warfare.

This was the year that I was promoted to Lieutenant Commander, which meant I would now wear two and one-half stripes and have more money to spend ($3,000 more for a total annual salary of $26,000). The latter was important because in September, Nanette Louise appeared at our house. We had not planned to have any more children after John, but to quote Robert Burns: "The best laid schemes o' mice and men gang aft a-gley." (A quotation often gives the reader the impression that the author is an intellectual, especially if part of the quote is in the Scottish dialect.)

Steve, 8, spent the year engrossed in space stories, astronomy and physical fitness. Doug started school that year and caught the learning bug while John mastered counting to 20, days of the week (not counting Thursday), and being completely enamored with baby Nanette.

Brother Will finished his tour at Stewart Air Force Base in Newburgh, NY, and headed for Vietnam in early December, and after spending three weeks and losing 20 pounds in survival training. We were all concerned about his safety in a combat zone, but flying as a bombardier-navigator in the B-58 Hustler was not comparable to the risk taken by the ground troops. We just knew he would not be a battle casualty.

The middle portion of the three-year tour at Pax River was mundane. There were a few aircraft accidents at the test center and Vietnam was heating up. The number of conscientious objectors and draft dodgers was growing exponentially, but the country, by and large continued to back the government in its efforts to prevent South

Vietnam from being overrun by communists.

The Wright family Christmas letter of 1966 highlighted the themed birthday parties of the boys, who turned 9, 7, and 5. Steve kicked it off in October with a secret agent party complete with coded invitations. Several of his invitees never showed up because they failed to break the code in time. John opted for a Batman soiree and turned our garage into a cave. An army theme was Doug's choice with sealed orders directing the recipients to come ready for war.

I was elected president of the PTA at the elementary school and attempted to convince myself that 33 was not too old to play organized sports. I played basketball for the WST intramural team, Sunday baseball for the St. Mary's County league, and touch football in the autumn that rounded out my obsession with athletics.

An excerpt from the local paper: "California continued to run away with the St. Mary's County Baseball League last Sunday as it whipped the perennial contenders for the flag, Tall Timbers, by a lopsided 11-5 score. Ted Greer, California center fielder, paced his team's attack with a single, a triple and a home run in four trips to the plate. He also scored three runs. Jim Gallimore pitched eight-hit ball and struck out seven batters to give the California its seventh straight win. Wright also came up with three hits including a double."

Here was a partial story from The Tester, a Navy publication produced on the base. The headline read: "WST Wins Pax I.M. Cage Crown." "A repeat of Thursday night's game? Hardly! All six of WST's players scored in double figures, set a high game scoring output with 95 points and made VP-8 wish they had deployed to Bermuda as they won the 1967 Station Intramural Basketball Championship in the title game last Friday night, 95-68. Guard Bob McAfee and forward Dick Macke combined for 50 points while Wright added 12 points, and Blackburn, Divito and Schrieber 10 points in gaining the victory for WST."

During the summer, Donna and I dropped off the children off at their grandparents' house in Northumberland, PA, and took a short New York City vacation. We saw two Broadway shows, "LUV" and "Cactus Flower," took a carriage ride in the park and spent too much money. We then attended my 15th high school reunion in Doylestown. The one memory that stands out in my mind was that the women were much more attractive than the men, probably because of premature balding and too much food consumed since high school. The other recollection was that the cliques that had existed in school were breaking down, and there was more camaraderie among classmates.

My youngest son, John, who had split and deformed his lip in 1965, had it operated on and had his handsome face restored. The Navy medical corps was excellent and had surgeons every bit as skilled as the finest in civilian life. Career military people took that benefit for granted.

By June of 1967, I had received orders to report to Helicopter Anti-Submarine Squadron Three, based in Norfolk, Virginia. Donna and the boys were pleased because it wasn't far away from Pennsylvania and it was technically in the Southern states, so the winters would not be too harsh.

We purchased a house at 3517 Bow Creek Blvd in Virginia Beach for $25,000 ($1200 down) and moved into the four bedroom home in July. It was about 20 miles to the base, but it was only a 25-minute trip to get to my new duty station in Norfolk. We thought we had 'arrived' since we could afford to purchase rather than rent our quarters. I was making $26,000 per year including flight pay.

In August I was off to Key West to learn to the fly the H-3 helicopter, despite the fact that I had been flying the H-3 for six straight years and had accumulated over 1,500 hours. There were no provisions in Navy policy to waive the requirement to report to a Replacement Air Group (RAG) and be taught to fly the fleet aircraft.

Twenty one flights (42 hours) later, which took two months to accomplish, I was back in Norfolk ready to 'keep the world safe for democracy' once more. I didn't object to spending sixty days in the RAG. I just thought it was too bad the Navy wasn't more flexible to waive the requirements that everyone must go through RAG training.

With flight time costing about $1,000 an hour, I thought the Navy could budget its money a little better.

So ended 1967 and my initial exposure to the world of testing. The Census Clock at the Commerce Department ticked past 200 million Americans.

CHAPTER 10

An East Coast Tour of Duty

*The only time an aviator has too much fuel is
when his aircraft is on fire.*

A SECOND SEA tour is unlike an initial assignment since you are now a mid-grade officer with a fleet reputation before reporting for duty. A number of pilots or aircrew will either know you or be familiar with your reputation before you arrive. Test pilots were usually not embraced with open arms by their fellow pilots in new squadrons. This animosity was caused by the attitude Patuxent River trained pilots conveyed to fleet pilots. The test pilots felt it was a step down in prestige to be attached to a fleet squadron after a tour at the Naval Air Test Center. They also believed that standardization rules were only guidelines and did not apply to real test pilots. It was no wonder that the welcome mat was absent when I reported to Helicopter Anti-Submarine Squadron Three (HS-3) in November 1967.

Since I was scheduled to be the maintenance officer in my new squadron, I delayed reporting until I had completed the two week Maintenance Management Information Systems course at Wright-Patterson Air Force Base in Dayton, Ohio. It was an interesting course with good instructors, but I'm not sure I learned too much about the 'nuts and bolts' of being a squadron maintenance officer. I received an 'A' for my efforts and recorded the required checkmark in the box.

Nine days later I reported to the temporary home of HS-3 in Naples, Italy, on board the USS Randolph, an aircraft carrier designated CVS.

Randolph had been a carrier that operated with fighter and attack aircraft in the past but was now utilized for anti-submarine warfare (ASW). That meant the fixed wing aircraft were slow moving S-2F propeller driven planes manufactured by Grumman and classified as old in aircraft-years. In addition, there were 16 SH-3 helicopters attached to the Air Group. All Air Groups deployed for six months at a time on an ASW carrier.

The usual complement of aviators was three per aircraft or 48 per helicopter squadron. The Commanding and Executive Officers were commanders (O-5), Marty Twite and George Rankin, respectively. The next in line were lieutenant commanders (Lcdrs) and there were usually eight to 10 per squadron. The eight Lcdrs. were Don Edmunds, Carl Megonigle, Bert Doe, Jim Magee, Bob Corbett, Stan Chiocchio, Bill Medlin, Harry Dews and me. Ten lieutenants held the remaining key jobs. Among them were Ron Jesberg, who would later make admiral, and Ben Bradberry, who would become a successful entrepreneur and writer. There were 20 lieutenant junior grade officers, including Bob Hanke and Wynn Montgomery. In addition, it was common to have several non-aviator-type officers assigned to the maintenance department. Only occasionally would an ensign make it through flight training and report to a fleet squadron before being promoted to Lt(jg). However, we had two ensigns, Larry Gemma and Jack Connell.

There were only two Lcdrs. senior to me when I initially joined HS-3. I received the distinct impression that they would teach me (the new guy) a lesson in humility by not recommending me to fly as helicopter aircraft commander (HAC) until six months had elapsed. To rub a little salt in the wounds, they assigned me to fly co-pilot with a brand new HAC, Lt(jg). John Hite. Even though I thought it wasn't professional, I simply went about my business and flew second seat until the required time period elapsed. By then I had logged a total of 1675 hours in the SH-3A helicopter, more than anyone else in the fleet.

I relieved Don Edmunds as Maintenance Officer immediately after reporting for duty and he took over as Operations Officer. My broad philosophy of leadership was to give subordinates as much authority as they were capable of handling. The vast majority of officers were delighted with that approach. I have always felt that the primary detractor in leading was letting one's ego get in the way and not giving credit to subordinates who actually deserved it. The truth is that the guys 'in the trenches' always knew the best way to efficiently solve problems. Supervisors often failed to get the best performance from their troops by discouraging any innovative approaches, or because they would rather do it 'the way we've always done it.'

Having returned from the Mediterranean Sea deployment in mid-December, the squadron spent all of 1968 stateside. There were several short deployments on a CVS while preparing for an extended six month cruise in mid-1969. No one minded the short (two or three week) at sea periods that were common during the 12 month period separating long cruises.

Because of the shortage of pilots coming through the training pipeline, the number of officers failing (washing out of) flight training was dramatically lower in the late 1960s. One beneficiary of lower grading standards was Fred Tolentino. He amassed six unsatisfactory flights (downs) during flight training but managed to acquire his wings of gold. He was sent to our squadron after completing SH-3 RAG training in Key West. We were informed that Fred was not a strong pilot before he reported to us for duty, but the unofficial Navy policy was to use all available manpower.

It turned out that Fred could not fly instruments to a satisfactory level, which was quite a disadvantage since the mission of ASW helicopter squadrons was to fly at night under instrument conditions to hunt for, and destroy enemy submarines. We would fly at a base altitude of 150 feet above sea level and transition into a 40 foot hover, at which time we would deploy our SONAR-dome into the water. There was not much room for error at such low altitudes.

In late April the Operations Officer, Don Edmunds, asked me to take Fred out on a series of flights and evaluate his ability to eventually fly as an aircraft commander with a crew and co-pilot under his charge. After some time spent in the ground trainer, I asked Fred to fly a series of maneuvers under instrument conditions and, with an open mike, tell me everything that was going through his mind as he flew these maneuvers. It turned out that his instrument scan, which should view just five basic flight instruments, consisted of watching all 30 instruments, even ones as unimportant as the main gearbox temperature. (I don't mean to imply that this information is not critical in some emergencies, but it should not be in a pilot's scan while flying precise profiles.) It was small wonder that he was having problems staying on altitude or airspeed. Fred also lacked some very basic knowledge, such as the definition of a radial. Since all positioning clearances are given in relation to radials, not knowing the definition of a radial is detrimental, the equivalent of navigating with a road map having no route numbers. I asked him how he had survived all the check rides he had been through without the requisite knowledge. He replied that he would turn one way and if he were wrong, the instructor would tell him to turn the other way. Unbelievable!

After studying the formula used by the Navy to determine aircraft availability, I concluded the most effective way to maximize your numbers was to ensure that on Friday you had as many aircraft as possible in a flight status so that they would remain in that status for both (non-flying) Saturday and Sunday. On my recommendation, HS-3 decided to fly only on Friday mornings. That way the maintenance department could restore the aircraft to flight status for the whole weekend. The end result was that our squadron led all the East Coast helicopter squadrons in aircraft availability. Since that was one of the primary measurements of performance among squadron commanding officers, it was a closely watched parameter. HS-3 was accused of manipulating availability numbers, but we didn't. Using this technique was somewhat inefficient since we didn't get as much flight time as other squadrons, but we had the highest readiness numbers.

In the spring of 1968, on the *Randolph*, our air group conducted a

119

six week anti-submarine exercise in South American waters, which meant crossing the equator, always a big adventure for shipboard personnel. By that time I had been across the equator four or five times, was one of the old time shellbacks, and had been involved in numerous initiations. I have always felt the rather sadistic exercise of using canvas shillelaghs to beat crawling 'pollywogs' on their derrieres was more appropriate in a college fraternity than a naval ship, but I bowed to two hundred years of tradition.

In early September HS-3 was tasked with supplying a four aircraft detachment to act as rescue helicopters for pilots requalifying on a carrier stationed at Naval Air Station Pensacola, Florida. Generally, with a mission of this type, the junior aviators were selected, both to add to their flight time as well as to give them a chance to demonstrate leadership qualities. The flight of four SH-3D helos took off from NAS Norfolk bound for Pensacola, with a refueling stop at Robins Air Force Base in Macon, Georgia. The first leg of the journey was uneventful with the exception of the fourth aircraft. It was designated the safety helicopter, with the task to ensure everyone in the flight flew in a prudent and safe manner. The safety aircraft took this opportunity to do some unauthorized low flying (flat-hatting) over several of the lakes they encountered en route. The pilot in command was Lt(jg). Harry "Wimpy" Wilkes and his co-pilot was Ensign Jack Connell.

After refueling with Air Force JP-4 (high octane jet fuel), the flight group took off on their final leg to Pensacola, Florida. Within 15 minutes of liftoff, the last aircraft in formation spotted a field that was being irrigated with several large agricultural spraying machines. The pilots decided to give their aircraft a wash by flying through the stream of water coming from the high-pressure nozzles. As they approached the spraying monsters, streams of water intersected from two of these giant fire hoses and struck the unsuspecting helicopter simultaneously. Both jet turbine engines immediately flamed out and the main rotor blades on the aircraft quickly slowed and stalled, sending the helicopter in a nose high, left wing down attitude. With the aircraft flying 50 feet above the ground when the engines quit, violent ground contact occurred two seconds later. The tail rotor blade struck the plowed cornfield first and the resultant force vector accelerated the fuselage into the ground with such a high 'g' force that it propelled both pilots through the cockpit windows, still strapped to their seats. The jet fuel ignited and the forward momentum of the flaming aircraft carried it directly over the co-pilot, who was instantly burned beyond recognition. Both crewmen perished immediately. The pilot in command miraculously survived the ordeal and returned to flight status about nine months later.

The following day I flew down to Georgia as senior member of the aircraft investigative board to determine the cause of the fatal accident. Although no one voluntarily disclosed the information immediately, it became obvious that the accident was caused by unbelievably poor pilot judgment. It turned out that this was not the first incident that this callow crew had experienced. On several occasions standard procedures were disregarded, and in one case, when the helicopter was in a 40 foot hover over the water, the co-pilot got out of his seat, opened the door and stood on the wheel covering (sponson) just for laughs. There were clear indications that we had failed to properly indoctrinate new pilots in command of their responsibilities. The result was the loss of three young men and a million dollar helicopter.

Wimpy regained consciousness the next day but was of no value to the investigating board since amnesia prevented him from remembering a single event after take off. I later learned that this is a common occurrence among accident victims. I asked the local flight surgeon whether anyone had relayed to the pilot that his entire crew had perished in the accident. The doctor replied that he thought I was the appropriate person to inform Wimpy of the sad news. When I passed on the tragic details to the pilot, his lack of surprise indicated he already suspected the worst. I cannot imagine what it's like to know you were responsible for the death of multiple shipmates through immature decision making.

After several months in the military hospital, Lt(jg). Wilkes returned to the squadron and was brought before a disciplinary board to determine what penalty would be imposed. The board was given great leeway and could recommend anything from revoking of wings to a Letter of Caution for his permanent record. Surprisingly, they opted for the minimum penalty and returned him to flight status. I think a factor in their decision was the fact that the Navy was having problems recruiting and retaining helicopter pilots.

The following month I was sent up to Halifax, Nova Scotia to attend a two week course in ASW tactics with emphasis on the coordinated employment of forces. All of my dealings with Canadian naval personnel have been quite positive. They never take themselves very seriously but they are quite professional in conducting military business.

In December I was relieved by Lcdr. Carl Megonigle as Maintenance Officer and took over as Operations Officer. Although I enjoyed my stint in the maintenance department, I felt more at home in operations. I liked the idea of having an impact on the way pilots trained and conducted flight operations at sea.

From a family perspective, 1968 was quite enjoyable. We lived in Virginia Beach, VA, and the weather was quite acceptable. There were some close calls involving bicycles, falling into creeks, and pushing the car out of the garage unsupervised with John (age 7) fearlessly behind the wheel but, no major mishaps occurred.

We did acquire a piano for $50 and paid another $100 to tune and repair it. Donna was the only member of the family that expressed any desire or interest in playing it. I purchased a tool kit and learned how to maintain our car, more out of frugality than interest in auto mechanics.

We took a short vacation to Kitty Hawk, North Carolina to see the spot where the Wright brothers made history some 65 years earlier. The kids loved wandering through our 'ancestral' stomping grounds.

One Sunday morning when our family arrived at church, John's Sunday school teacher approached us and stated she had some good news. "John has agreed to sit down," she declared. It seems that after his first week in Sunday school, classes had changed and John was required to go to a new classroom. He was miffed at the idea and refused to sit for the following six weeks. This incident should have been an indicator of things to come. John also lectured Nanette (age 4) that she needed work on her consonant blends.

I recall receiving a request from a county official in Georgia to put one of our helicopters on display at a county fair. It was not an unusual request and it was Navy policy to create as positive an impression as possible with the general public, if it did not interfere with our flight operations or impact availability. This display would be on the weekend and two pilots from Georgia volunteered to make the flight on their own time. The two pilots were Lt(jg). Bill Burnett and Lt(jg). Bill Ladson. Both recently had attained their HAC qualifications.

I later found out they slightly exaggerated some facts to the visiting public, as printed in the local newspaper. They announced that the particular helicopter on display picked up astronauts on the recent space recovery with the very rescue harness (horse collar) connected to the hoist on this aircraft. People were lined up as far as the eye could see to have their picture snapped in the 'astronauts'' rescue sling. When some cub scouts came to tour the helicopter, one of the pilots told them the pilot's relief tube was a public address system. Many cub scouts shouted through the tube, simulating instructions to people in the water being rescued. The young pilots thought the whole episode was hilarious. It could have been a public relations disaster. I was much more selective after this incident in choosing pilots to fly to an unsupervised event.

An aircraft squadron is quite unlike a business corporation. There are similarities but no company can hope to create a band of brothers' mindset that is an inherent part of a squadron family. That is not to say that there are not disagreements among the brothers or that some of the brothers use bad judgment some of the time. They do. But, since the aircrew trusts their lives to one another, there is a special relationship. These remarks are made to show that military organizations get involved in each other's personal lives considerably more than colleagues working for a civilian company. This is especially true when aircraft accidents result in the death of young talented men in the prime of their lives. The year 1969 was to be a tragic one in my life in a very personal way.

The year started in a fairly typical manner. I was the Officer in Charge (OIC) of a six aircraft detachment to Naval Station Roosevelt Roads in Puerto Rico. Norfolk based helicopter squadrons would deploy to places like 'Roosy Roads' to avail themselves of submarine services, which were in short supply in the continental United States. We would often get a four or eight hour period to track friendly submarines, primarily at night. It was a great opportunity for junior officers to build up their nighttime flight hours and get experience prosecuting actual submarines that would maneuver to avoid detection.

Lt(jg). Wimpy Wilkes, fresh from rehabilitation following his accident, was part of the detachment. He came to me about dusk one evening almost in tears. He had told the detachment operations officer, Lcdr. Jim Magee, that he didn't feel up to flying that evening. Jim replied that he should turn in his wings then and find some other line of business. I interceded and gave Wimpy the night off, but warned him that if he wanted to be a naval aviator, he had to fly his scheduled flights and overcome his fears. My reasoning was that the trauma he had gone through was sufficient without the humiliation of being forced to turn in his wings. He was getting out of the Navy shortly after our detachment returned to Norfolk anyway, so I thought let's not create unnecessary ill will. He flew the following night without incident and I smoothed the ruffled feathers that Magee had for me for not backing his decision.

In August of 1969, Helicopter Antisubmarine Squadron 3 flew their SH-3D helicopters aboard the USS Yorktown (CVS-10) in Norfolk, Virginia and set sail due East for a six month deployment to the North Atlantic. We visited ports in France, Germany, Denmark, and England. The ship also crossed the Arctic Circle, permitting all hands to call themselves 'Blue Noses.' One might think that heavy seas would not have that much impact on a 40,000 ton carrier, but when the wind gets up to Force 10 (winds of 50 knots and waves over 30 feet high), no one on board thinks of anything except survival. Flight operations cease and all hands are warned to stand clear of all weather decks. Half of the crew is seasick and the other half is not concerned about killing submarines. Fortunately, running into such foul weather is unusual since the ship's navigator does his best to avoid stormy areas. High seas are encountered about once every deployment.

Barely three weeks into the cruise, HS-3 had their first crisis. On September 18, 1969, SH-3D 152698 flew into the water immediately after take-off from Yorktown at 2200 hours (10 p.m.). It was a dark night and the aircraft was lined up perpendicular (270 relative degrees) to the ship's runway. Upon liftoff, the pilots had no visible reference to judge the helicopter's attitude and Lt. Fred Tolentino flew his aircraft into the water, nose down. Only the plane commander, Lt. Wayne Reeve, sitting in the left seat, survived the crash. The subsequent investigation, in which I was the senior member of the accident board, revealed that an error was made in the preflight checks (the Automatic Stabilization Equipment control knob was left in the full down position), which resulted in the aircraft having no stabilization in the pitch axis upon liftoff. Fred became distracted with the ASE problem and failed to realize that his aircraft was in a severe nose down attitude as he collided with the water. The accident report also found the Yorktown at fault for not aligning the helicopter with the deck runway, which would have given the pilot a visual reference after takeoff, thereby allowing him to establish a positive climb rate before transitioning to instrument flight.

Fatal accidents always have a painful effect on a squadron, for obvious reasons. When the incident occurs on cruise, the impact on those dependents left at home is multiplied because there is already a high stress level without husbands to share family responsibilities. Wives and children often live in fear that their aircrew husbands/fathers are never coming home after departing on deployment. Another distress factor is there is no one around to explain exactly what caused the accident. Who was responsible? Who was driving? Why did they crash? Why my husband?

At times like these 'A Fighter Pilot's Prayer' comes to mind. "Lord, I pray for the eyes of an eagle, the heart of a lion, and the courage of a combat helicopter pilot. Amen."

On October 9th I was awakened by the executive officer, who told me my scheduled night flight was cancelled because my brother, Wilbur, was killed in a B-52 accident at Castle Air Force Base in California. The next morning I was on a carrier on board delivery (COD) plane en route to Scotland for further transfer to a transatlantic flight to Dover, Delaware.

The burial was at Arlington Cemetery in a moving and emotional service. His widow, Annette, my Dad, and many Tabor alumni attended. Sister Wilma drove a van down to Virginia with Don and Marty Fritz, Dotty Buckner, and Carl Hoppe. Skip Yerkes, Ralph Michner, and Lee Robinson were also in attendance. It was a surreal moment, as accidental death often is. The sickening realization that I would never see Will again would come somewhat later. Dad was grief stricken and it was the first time I had ever seen him in distress. I thought how I would react if my wife and two of my three children would all die before the age of 35. It was too hard to contemplate so I spent my time tending to the grieving guests.

Military men react to death quite differently than their civilian counterparts. It is part of an aviator's world. No one dwells on death but every pilot accepts the fact that the possibility of 'buying the farm' is part of the program you sign up for. So, when I learned of Will's demise, there were no tears or depression. He had outwitted the system when he memorized the eye chart to become a bombardier-navigator and was a victim of an unskilled 'rookie' aviator. He certainly didn't deserve to die but he joined the ranks of those patriots that gave all.

Will's obituary mentioned that he earned the Distinguished Flying Cross, two Air Medals, and the Vietnam Service Medal with three Bronze Stars. Survivors included his widow Annette, a daughter Yvonne, and a stepson Christen.

The circumstances surrounding Wilbur's death were straight-forward. He had completed a tour in Viet Nam with nary a scratch to show for his numerous combat flights as an electronic warfare officer. He was stationed at March Air Force Base at Riverside, California but was undergoing training at Castle Air Force Base at the time of the accident. After completing a routine night training flight, the B-52 bomber was practicing touch and go landings and takeoffs when one of the student copilots caught a wing and the aircraft cart wheeled down the runway coming to rest about one thousand feet north of the runway. The eight jet engines were scattered throughout the charred area with the wreckage strewn over several acres. Six officers were killed including two student co-pilots.

A letter to the editor of the Doylestown Intelligencer from Ralph Michner, a teacher and coach at Central Bucks High School seemed to capture the moment.

"Will" Wright, Class of '53, CBHS

To The Editor

The scene was in the old Doylestown Armory late in February 1950. It was a playoff game between two junior high basketball teams for the Bux-Mont Junior League championship of that year. At the end of three quarters, Souderton Junior High was leading by nine points and the loyal followers of old Doylestown Junior High were about ready to toss in the towel of defeat. But in the fourth quarter one of the Doylestown boys got 'hot.' And, as his teammates fed him the ball, this boy made basket after basket, most of them long, two handed set shots from far out on the floor. As time ran out, a final shot by this boy brought a one point victory to the Doylestown team. After the game, in congratulating the Doylestown coach, Bill Maza, the Souderton coach said, "That boy, Wright, really won the game for you!" Needless to say, this same coach enjoyed the privilege of asso-ciating with Wilbur Wright, and his brother, Orville, in the classroom as well as in athletics.

Both of the Wright brothers, raised in Tabor Home under the

dedicated guidance of Sister Wilma, were to go on to become graduates of the U.S. Naval Academy at Annapolis. They advanced in rank and they served their country honorably and well in their chosen profession. "Will" became a captain in the U.S. Air Force, and Orville, the older brother, a lieutenant commander in the U.S. Navy.

And now, Captain "Will" is dead! On October 8th, a plane crash at Castle Air Force Base, Merced, California, took the life of this one, who, as a boy and man, was a loyal American, a good citizen, husband and father to his wife, Annette and their two children.

When the 15th reunion of the class of 1954, Central Bucks High School, took place last Saturday evening, at the William Penn Inn, Gwynedd Valley, this joyous occasion was tempered by the knowledge of the tragedy which had occurred just three days before to this honored and respected member of the preceding class, the class of 1953. As guests at this reunion, Mr. And Mrs. Arthur Reese, my good wife and I, could join with the members of '54 in our memories of "Will" Wright, Class of '53.

"Will" Wright is dead, but his memory will remain in the hearts and lives of the many who will be inspired to be better and more loyal citizens of this great land of ours because he has lived. Certainly, the original Wright brothers, Wilbur and Orville, the first successful flyers of a heavier than air plane, would be proud of their later name sakes, our own Wilbur and Orville, who have followed them so successfully and so well.

One of the old teachers and coaches of the Wright brothers. (signed) Ralph Michner, Doylestown

To keep the memory of Will alive, I decided to set up a memorial award consisting of a medal and a cash award of $250 (equivalent to $1638 in 2019 dollars) to the Central Bucks High School athlete voted 'most outstanding for three years in interscholastic competition.' Don Fritz, Will's best friend, was designated treasurer of the fund. The award was to last at least 10 years and the first recipient was John Harbison, a first year student at Thiel College in Greenville, PA, in 1970. I would like to report that contributions rolled in and the memorial award was a huge success. In fact, the National Collegiate Athletic Association (NCAA) got wind of the award and sent us a letter stating any cash award given to any college athlete would result in that student being declared a professional and thereby ineligible to participate in any collegiate sport. The best laid plans of mice and men ....

As I look at the squadron roster consisting of 50 officers, I am struck by the fact that after 43 years, I have run into only a handful after I left HS-3. Jim Magee retired and was hired by a 'beltway bandit.' (The nickname given to defense contractors who have offices in and around Washington, D.C.) Bob Hanke ended up with a responsible position in NavAir in Washington, and Wynn Montgomery was the naval representative at IBM in the early 1980s, so I saw him and his wife Carolyn socially for a number of years. I ran into Dave Speidel several times while visiting Tabor Home. Dave ended up living and working near Doylestown and put me in touch with Ben Bradberry, who had just finished writing his memoirs, which I found very interesting. Through Ben, I connected with Stan Chiocchio, who was living in New Orleans and fighting some major health problems.

By year end I had received orders to report to the Flight Test Division, Naval Air Test Center at Naval Air Station Patuxent River, MD. My tour with HS-3 was over and I was looking forward to two years at NATC testing aircraft once again. Little did I know what was in store for me concerning my command tour of duty.

CHAPTER 11

Patuxent River and Commanding HS-8

You know you have landed with the wheels up
if it takes full power to taxi to the ramp.

RETURNING TO PAX River for a second shore tour was desirable on several counts. I was back in my element of testing helicopters and their electronic systems and we were assigned base housing. The children were still in school in Virginia Beach so we chose to delay the family moving until the school year was complete. I chose to live in the Bachelor Officers Quarters on the base, commuting home on Fridays and back on Sunday evenings.

One such evening I learned, for the first time, that there is a basic difference between males and females (other than the obvious biological factors). Prior to heading back to Pax River, I was writing checks to pay some weekly bills. Donna, for reasons unknown to me, wanted to argue about some incidental subject. I explained I had to finish this task and, if she persisted, I would finish the job upstairs. She continued and I retreated up the stairs. Donna immediately started crying loudly which resulted in 4-year-old Nanette hurrying to the second floor. Than she said, "When you come downstairs, will you tell Mommy you're sorry?"

"Sorry for what?" I replied, irritated.

"For making her cry," was her response.

"Alright, I will," I said half-heartedly.

Sensing a success, Nanette descended the stairs and reported, "Daddy said he was sorry."

"That's not good enough," was her immediate reply.

Back up the stairs marched the peace maker. "Could you bring Mommy a present?"

"I don't have any presents up here."

"No. Bring her a present when you come home next week."

Frustrated that I was being outwitted by a child, I replied, "OK, maybe I will get her a present."

Her final statement was, "When you are picking out Mommy's present, you know those dolls that smile and frown? Can you buy one for me?"

I suddenly realized that from birth, the minds of females function differently than males. The boys' attitude toward feigned tears for manipulation would have been, "Mom, stuff it!"

I suspected the transition from sea to shore duty as a commander would be positive, but the effect it had on the family came as a surprise. Our base housing consisted of a one acre, three-story house enclosed within a six-foot high hedge. It was minutes away from work and the kids loved the freedom the base afforded them. The large gymnasium, containing an Olympic sized swimming pool, was walking distance from our front door. Free bus service was available all over the base and there were high performance combat aircraft that constantly made low level passes across our yard. What could be better for young boys between eight and twelve years old?

The tour was defined as two years since I had screened for command of Helicopter Anti-Submarine Squadron Four, presently commanded by an old friend and shipmate of mine, Warren Aut. My professional future was looking bright and my long term goal of making flag rank appeared doable. Little did I know that a seemingly unrelated event was going to complicate my military future.

The year was 1970 and the country of 203 million people was divided ideologically. Anti-war protests were common as draft age young men attempted to avoid that letter from the President that many thought was a death notice. During one such protest, students at Kent State University were fired on by the local National Guard troops resulting in the death of four protesters. One strategy, to avoid the draft, was to enlist in the Navy or Air Force (few chose the Marines since boot camp was way too challenging). Fleeing to Canada was another evasion option even though this decision would result in a felony on one's record. A more drastic approach was to actually shoot oneself in the foot. Not many logical thinkers chose this route. In any case, the country was in chaos. The My Lai massacre was front and center with 14 Army officers charged with a cover up or at least suppressing vital information. The tide had turned and the general consensus was that the country was tired of Vietnam and we wanted our boys home. By November, the war was winding down with no casualties that month. The nightmare appeared over.

One of my duties as a member of the Rotary Wing Branch was to give presentations to 'visiting firemen' on field trips to the test center. During one of my presentations to 40 midshipmen and their officer representative on aircraft procurement, I created a scenario whereby a defense contractor (portrayed by a GS-14 civilian employee) delivered a new weapon system (in this case an ASW helicopter). I tested it and described the deficiencies to the contractor as we debated about who would fix the discrepancies and who would pay for them. Following the conclusion of the briefing, the officer representative of the visiting Naval Academy class took the 'defense contractor' to task and berated him for 'delivering the Navy a defective product.' Evidently, he missed the part about role playing. The admiral sent a letter of appreciation the following week with these words.

"On Wednesday, 22 April 1970, a group of 40 midshipmen and one faculty member from the Division of Aerospace Engineering made a field trip to the Naval Air Test Center for briefings at the Test Pilot School and Flight Test Division. The trip was in support of class work in stability and control. It was proposed to show how knowledge gained in course work could be applied to the solution of practical problems. The afternoon was spent at the Flight Test Division where pertinent lectures were given by officers of each branch. An ingenious presentation, staged by Commander Wright of the Rotary Wing Branch, gave the midshipmen a real insight into the problems the Navy faces when procuring new aircraft."

That year the navy chartered a new squadron consisting of mine sweeping H-53 helicopters. With Hai Phong Harbor full of mines and the war winding down, it seemed probable that part of the peace negotiations would be for the United States to take responsibility to clear those mines. Helicopters were more efficient at sweeping mines than traditional wooden hulled boats with less risk of being damaged by the mine exploding. Since all the helicopter officers that had screened for command had been tentatively assigned to squadrons, there was a temporary shortage of qualified pilots to fill the void. The class desk officer contacted me and stated he would like me to move up a year and start my executive officer year 12 months early with a different squadron. When I questioned the decision, he replied the Bureau of Personnel could not guarantee I would get any squadron to command if I didn't cooperate and accept their decision to change orders. Several facts were not obvious to me at the time. First, having a friend as a commanding officer is a huge plus in the competitive world of military hierocracy. (In this case promotion to captain, O-6). Secondly, accelerating your command tour puts you at the bottom of the totem pole regarding your post-command assignment. In my case, the executive officer of the LPH New Orleans, a commander I was competing with for O-6, was filling out my fitness report. So, in December 1970, I saluted smartly and reported as executive officer of Helicopter Anti-Submarine Squadron Eight, home based at Naval Air Station Imperial Beach, CA under the command of Commander T. David Eyres.

The year 1971 was a mess! A nation wide poll indicated 59 percent of the public thought the U.S. made a mistake by sending troops to fight in Vietnam. There would be 2,357 more combat deaths as the year progressed. Anti-war militants flooded Washington D.C. and 12,000 were arrested. The Supreme Court ruled that busing of students may be ordered to achieve racial desegregation. The Pentagon Papers were published and the 26th amendment to the Constitution, which lowered the voting age from 21 to 18, was passed. The president was Richard Nixon and his VP was Spiro Agnew, but not all the news was bad.

The third successful moon landing was achieved with astronauts Alan Shepard, Stuart Roosa, and Edgar Mitchell participating. Gasoline was selling for 40 cents a gallon and the median household income was just over $9,000. Life expectancy was 71 years and the federal debt $408 billion. Unemployment was under five percent and the Postal Service raised the price of a first class stamp in May from six to eight cents.

In January, HS-8, along with Carrier Anti-Submarine Air Group 59, embarked on the USS Ticonderoga (CVS-14) for a six month deployment to the Western Pacific. They flew Sikorsky SH-3D 'Sea King' helicopters with a mission of anti-submarine warfare (ASW). ASW exercises were conducted in the Philippine Sea, Gulf of Tonkin, Indian Ocean, Sea of Japan, the North Pacific, and Bearing Sea. Ports of call were Subic Bay in the Philippines, Sasebo and Yokosuka in Japan, and Hong Kong, where many wives travelled to welcome their husbands, including my wife Donna. She commented that she had no fear when walking around the city because the men were so small.

While deployed, the Commanding Officers (COs) and Executive Officers (XOs) in the air group dined at separate tables for evening meals. During one meal the subject of discussion was carrying out of any of your CO's plans with which you disagreed and thought foolish. If you thought the idea was foolish, how do you convey the task to the troops? Of seven XOs at the table, six stated they would execute the plans as if it were coming from them, thereby protecting the CO from criticism. My position was to try to have the CO change his position, but if that was unsuccessful, I would tell the troops where the order came from and that we would carry it out. I was clearly in the minority regarding leadership techniques in the chain of command. My feeling was that the troops are quite discerning and they will know when their boss disagrees with his boss and they will respect you more if you express your opinion while still motivating their staff to implement the decision. A leader must be true to himself and to his troops.

The year as XO passed swiftly and without any serious incidents. One early event stands out as I recall the year. The CO had invited all the officers to his house for a pool party. Sensing that the venue was ideal to welcome the new XO (me) by throwing him in the water, I suggested to several of the junior officers (JOs) that we sign a self-protection pact and that an attack on one would constitute an attack on us all. When the inevitable hour arrived, the JOs lived up to their agreement and defended me against the perpetrators. The aggressive pilots who planned the 'sneak attack' were stunned that junior officers would defend a senior officer. Tabor Home training had paid off once more!

From the moment I was sworn in at the Naval Academy, there were situations that puzzled me. Why would senior officers make life at Annapolis so disheartening, that after four years of training, few wanted to make the Navy a career, and almost no one looked forward to life at sea? During flight training, where students would actually risk their lives learning to fly, why did everyone cheer when inclement weather grounded all the aircraft? There had to be a better way to train. After arriving in the fleet, why wasn't there higher esprit de corps among the troops? Why were reenlistment rates among enlisted men in the single digits? Why wasn't it fun to 'Join the navy and see the world?' I couldn't wait to institute a better way to lead. On October 1971 I was sworn in as Commanding Officer, Helicopter Anti-Submarine Squadron Eight.

Just as one doesn't get to pick their parents, commanding officers do not get to pick their second in command. I was fortunate to have as my XO, Cdr. Paul Caine, a rock solid helicopter pilot from

Missoula, Montana who loved to fly and was as loyal as the day was long. His wife, Nancy, was the embodiment of a naval officer's wife, competent, caring, and independent, while convincing her husband he was in charge. Lcdr. Rich Franks was the Operations Officer, another top notch officer, who would be selected to command HS-2 in 1975. Lcdr. Walt Lester, a strong advocate for naval helicopter aviation, ran the maintenance department in a professional manner, and Lt. Mack Thomas was Quality Assurance and later commanded HS-8. Even the newest pilots to report, like Mark Vanderberg (a very good tennis player and later CO of HS-5) and Bill Cain, were impressive from the start. Lt. Jim Mosser did a bang-up job as NATOPS (standardization) officer and was an excellent pilot, but he did not suffer fools gladly. I counseled him that he was competent enough to make flag rank, but because of his abrupt manner, he might not make it to lieutenant commander.

The point I am trying to make is that no matter how good the coach is, one has to have high performers for the team to be successful, and we did. HS-8 ended the year with the highest Operational Evaluation score on the West Coast. We also more than doubled the next highest reenlistment rate of all HS and VS squadrons in the Navy. With the average reenlistment rate hovering about six percent, I'm not saying that our 20 percent was world class, but remember Vietnam was still active and few were clamoring to enlist in the service.

Several events occurred in 1972 that were significant. I invited the mayor of San Diego, Pete Wilson (who later was elected governor and a shining star in the Republican Party) to speak at the Ream Field Officers' Club. Because of his scheduling commitments, he was unable to meet our timetable using ground transportation. I went up my chain of command to the Air Group Commander and got permission to fly him by helicopter to make the meeting. Everything went well. I gave him an extensive introduction and he followed with a very interesting talk about the political life of a mayor of a major city in the Sunshine State of California. All appeared rosy until a letter to the editor in the *San Diego Union* newspaper asked why the military was flying politicians around at taxpayer's expense? The answer was a Letter of Caution in my jacket from Commander Fleet Air San Diego to Commanding Officer, HS-8, entitled "Embarkation of unauthorized passengers in naval aircraft." It further went on, "Although this trip fell within the broad spectrum of persons eligible for such a flight, the dictums pertaining to approval authority were not met. This Headquarters is not adverse to this type of endeavor, however, deviations from prescribed procedures will not be tolerated."

The Air Group Commander, R.W. Kennedy, endorsed the letter as follows, "Your diligence, initiative, and devotion to duty is viewed with growing alarm!" It was obvious that my boss treated the Letter of Caution as a joke.

After I took over as CO of HS-8, I made it clear to all pilots that they should treat flying as a profession. Practice emergency procedures, master all aspects of your aircraft, and follow the standardization manual because it was written in blood by survivors that determined the best way to prosecute submarines. By knowing the correct procedures, they would be able to judge when to deviate from them. Sometimes it would be necessary to do so. "You are the bull fighter and you, alone, are charged with fighting the bull, regardless of what the critics say, sitting in the arena. If you act in the best interests of the squadron or the Navy, I will back you 100 percent. But, if you chose to deviate for personal reasons and decide to perform unauthorized maneuvers like flat hatting, you won't get my support."

In the spring of 1972, HS-8, with eight helicopters and 24 pilots, got underway as part of Carrier Air Group 59, for a six month deployment to the Western Pacific. After several weeks in Hawaii, practicing anti-submarine tactics with U.S. submarines, we deployed off the coast of Vietnam and in the Sea of Japan. We operated around the clock with a six hour cycle requiring one night HIFR (helicopter in flight refueling), which consisted of hovering for 10 to 15 minutes over the fantail of a destroyer as they topped us off with jet fuel. Keep in mind that ASW helicopters operate from a base altitude of 150 feet down to a 40 foot hover when the active SONAR transducer is deployed. It was intense flying and required maximum concentration. In the contact area, fixed wing aircraft (S-2s), utilizing sonobuoys and MAD (magnetic anomaly detector) equipment, were used to classify and possibly attack enemy submarines using depth charges or torpedoes. They operated from 200 feet to 400 feet above sea level so it was obvious that altitude discipline was absolutely required to avoid mid air collisions. To an outside observer, prosecuting submarines at night may appear to be total chaos, but to a well trained team, it was like an intricate circus act.

Half way through the deployment, one of the S-2 commanders made a recommendation to the ship's captain that the six hour flight cycle be increased to a seven hour cycle since the fixed wing could fly more efficiently. The downside of the more efficient cycle would be increasing the number of night HIFRs by one. Both commanding officers of the helicopter squadrons strenuously objected to the Air Group Commander on safety grounds. He arranged a meeting with the ship's CO to consider our concerns. The other helicopter CO, Cdr. Trig Trygsland, asked me to be the spokesman. I agreed and laid out the case for not extending the cycle, since we both thought our aircrews were operating right on edge of safety presently, due to excess fatigue and stress. The ship's CO listened but stated he was going to institute the change in spite of our reservations. Cdr. Trygsland immediately responded, 'Aye, aye, sir' and turned to leave. I said, "Captain, if any of my pilots are killed due to this decision, I will report to the accident board the result of this meeting." The ship's captain was up for advancement to admiral (O-7) shortly and there was no way he was going to risk being passed over for something as mundane as increasing a cycle time for 'damned' helicopters. He dismissed us with the comment that he would take our concerns under advisement. I knew I had convinced him to change his decision. There was no way I could face a grieving widow, knowing I had put my promotion concerns ahead of her husband's life. My career was over but it was one of the easiest decisions of my life. The captain backed down; we lost no pilots; I was rated 'last of seven among all commanding officers in the

Air Group' and the captain was passed over for admiral. Incidentally, Trygsland was evaluated one of seven and was selected for captain. He died of a heart attack several years after retirement.

On November 17, 1972, I was relieved by Cdr.Paul Caine with orders to relieve Ed Benshop as 'Air Boss' on the USS New Orleans (LPH-11) operating out of San Diego.

CHAPTER 12

Air Boss on the
USS New Orleans (LPH-11)

Will Rogers said, "We can't all be heroes because somebody
has to sit on the curb and clap as they go by."

A SHIPBOARD POST command tour is critical for any commander who aspires to captain or flag officer rank. Specific billets are designated to be filled by officers who have just completed their tours as commanding officer (CO) of an aircraft squadron. Fighter and attack COs are ordered to large carriers as navigators, operations officers, air officers or executive officers. Officers who commanded S-2 squadrons (fixed wing anti-submarine) would serve in similar billets on ASW carriers. Helicopter post command tours were served on LPH-type ships (amphibious assault) that housed combat Marines and Marine Helicopter Squadrons. The three designated billets were executive, operations, and air officers.

The *New Orleans* was commissioned in 1968, the sixth Iwo Jima class amphibious assault ship, so it was relatively new when I reported aboard in 1973. It was 600 feet long, 100 feet wide, had two engines, two elevators, one propeller, and displaced almost 20,000 tons while generating 22,000 shaft horsepower. With a maximum speed of just over 20 knots, it was not going to win any races with destroyers that were capable of exceeding 30 knots. It was designed to transport fully equipped Marine assault troops into combat areas and land them by helicopters. The ship was also capable of supporting mine-sweeping operations with Helicopter Mine Counter-Measures Squadrons. With Marines on board, we generally deployed with 20 CH-46D helicopters and 1,750 troops. Ship's company consisted of 80 officers and 640 enlisted men.

I was fortunate to have the best job on the ship, 'air boss,' responsible for the safe conduct of flight operations for the next two years. I was accustomed to dealing with helicopter pilots who thought that shipboard operators were out to kill them. 'Don't trust anyone' was a common belief among Navy pilots when operating aboard ship. I was in for a shock the first time I interacted with Marine pilots. They exhibited a fearless, unwarranted faith that they were immune from death. Two examples should make the case. During flight operations, we kept track of all aircraft airborne and how long they had been aloft. When questioned about their state (fuel remaining) it was usually given in minutes remaining before they start returning to the ship. Early in the deployment, I asked one Marine helo for a state report. He quickly replied, "Zero plus 20." Incredulous, I inquired whether that was to splash (time until he completely ran out of fuel)?

"Affirmative," was his response.

"You are cleared to return and land immediately," was my frantic reply.

I could not believe that any pilot would rely on a fuel gauge that indicated he would have to ditch his aircraft in the ocean in 20 minutes and not be concerned. And I had to initiate the call!

The second event involved a flight of two helicopters cleared to transit to the beach, bearing 270 (West) degrees. They took off and flew 090 (East) degrees heading out to sea. Thinking there was a reason for the deviation, I delayed calling them for about ten minutes.

"Call Sign 151, what are your intentions? You are heading due East out to sea."

After a few minutes the answer came back, "Sorry sir, my magnetic compass had not stabilized."

I later talked to the pilot (Marine captain) of the second aircraft about the snafu. "When were you going to tell the lead he was going in the wrong direction?"

"It was up to the major to figure it out, not me," came back the reply.

At that point I realized I had better be on my toes if I didn't want a disaster on my watch. Fortunately, I had a very able assistant, Lcdr. Bob Wildman, who had at least a year's worth of experience in the tower dealing with Marine aviators.

The primary helicopter that the Marine Corps squadrons flew on the New Orleans was the CH-46D Sea Knight, a medium lift, tandem rotor, with two T-58 turbo shaft engines generating 1400 shaft horse power each. They could carry 25 troops or 7,000 pounds of cargo. They are especially useful for vertical lift operations but the Marines used them for combat support, search and rescue, and casualty evacuation. Being a Marine helicopter pilot in the combat zone flying H-46 helicopters during the Vietnam War was not a formula for longevity, since over 100 Sea Knights were shot down by enemy fire during the war.

The assigned missions during my ship-borne tour were recovering astronauts in Sky Lab 3 and 4, supporting removal of mines in Hai Phuong Harbor in North Vietnam, transporting peace negotiators attempting to end the war, and operating off the coast of Vietnam with combat Marines. At no time was I exposed to enemy fire, although kids did throw rocks at our helo while transporting negotiators into North Vietnam. The two officers commanding New Orleans were Captain Robert W. Carius, a Naval Academy graduate, and Captain Ralph E. Neiger. I had a professional relationship with both COs and they seemed pleased with my performance as air boss. In my view, they were both competent officers but neither was selected for admiral (O-7). Being skipper of an LPH was not high on the pecking order of billets for selection to flag rank.

One event stood out in my mind when we were undergoing

a workup for recovery of the capsule in Sky Lab 3. While rehearsing maneuvering of the ship in an arbitrary designated time frame, Captain Carius put himself on report to a remote headquarters, a thousand miles away, stating he had exceeded the allotted time to get to a specific location for capsule retrieval. It was only one of a dozen attempts and I felt the admission of a 'failure' was unnecessary and foolish.

Sky Labs 3 and 4 were conducted in 1973 and 1974, respectively, to study the effects of weightlessness on human beings in a zero-gravity environment. Sky Lab 3 lasted 59 days and Sky Lab 4 increased the time limits to 84 days. There were no speeches, no red carpets, and the Navy band played for only about a minute. After the splashdown on target in the Pacific, 225 miles southwest of San Diego, the three astronauts were whisked to the deck of the recovery carrier New Orleans. Then, wobbly but smiling, they were guided by NASA doctors a few steps to waiting chairs and quickly carted off atop a moving platform for medical examinations. The return of Skylab 3 Astronauts Alan Bean, Jack Lousma, and Owen Garriott was in fact so subdued compared to past homecomings that it did not begin to do justice to their remarkable accomplishments; they had just completed man's longest voyage in space!

Here is how the Doylestown Intelligencer saw the event. They headlined "Bucks Flier Helps Skylab." "When Skylab 3's command module burst back into the earth's atmosphere Tuesday, a Doylestown native and Central Bucks High School graduate with an appropriate flyer's name was right down below watching. Not only was Cdr Orville Wright aboard the aircraft carrier USS New Orleans, but the 39 year old product of Tabor Home for Children and the U.S. Naval Academy was the air officer controlling all of the big ship's air activity.

It was Wright's first participation in the recovery of astronauts, and he was impressed, he said Thursday morning in a long distance phone conversation from San Diego, California, where astronauts Alan Bean, Jack Lousma, and Owen Garriott were preparing to disembark from the New Orleans.

Although the capsule landed upside down in the 10 to 12 foot seas, it was quickly righted and there were no hitches at all, said Wright, who was also in charge of loading the command module onto the vessel and getting it off again in San Diego.

Wright said the recovery team is given a maximum of 60 minutes to haul the space crew aboard, the reason being that scientists are in a hurry to start testing while the astronauts are fresh from the heavens."

Skylab 4 was recovered in February 1974 with three astronauts (Ed Gibson, Gerald Carr, and Bill Pogue) on board. After 84 days in earth orbit, the three men were constantly reminded that adjusting to terrestrial life was not without perils and problems. Once familiar sights and sounds now seemed exceedingly strange. Though their initial dizziness soon passed, every physical effort was a chore. Pogue, who said he felt as if he weighed a thousand tons, found that it even was work to roll over in bed. When Carr rested his head in his wife's lap, he kept asking if it was too heavy for her. For 21 days the astronauts were required to continue to eat Skylab-type prepackaged food, a tee totaling, less than gourmet diet that was particularly hard on Commander Carr. As expected, the three men almost immediately lost the one to two inches in height that they had gained in orbit; without any weight on the spinal column, the spaces between the vertebrae had expanded. The only really puzzling physical effect of the long tour was the loss of red blood cells and blood plasma, though it was less than that of other crews. There was a growing conviction that there may be no practical limits on how long man can live in space.

During the 1974 deployment to the Western Pacific, our mission was quite different from the previous year's cruise, which consisted of Marine assault troops and a full complement of CH-46D combat helicopters. In March of that year, the U.S. pulled their troops out of Vietnam. This mission called for transporting and supporting MH-53 mine sweeping helicopters, equipped with various devices to de-mine the harbors in North Vietnam. We knew, of course, the location of all of the active mines but we were in no big hurry to efficiently sweep them clean. The primary device used was a magnetized pole which would be dragged behind the helicopter and act as a ship decoy, fooling the mine into exploding. Under the Geneva Convention Laws, all mines must have a specified life, after which they self-implode. By the time we started de-mining, there was only one mine still active in the harbor.

On the surface, one might think that a helicopter mine sweeping mission is quite safe since the airspeed is so slow. However, the low altitude and extreme nose-down pitch creates a serious emergency in the event of an engine failure. One of our H-53 helicopters suffered such a failure and struck the water in a nose-down attitude. The pilot was face down in the water, unconscious and seconds away from drowning when the ship's life boat crew, that was en route to the beach, rescued the pilot. Their quick actions definitely saved his life. During the peace negotiations, we volunteered to clear all the mines in the adjacent rivers. The North Vietnamese negotiators did not want any Americans in their country so we just supplied the 'magnetic' poles, conveniently failing to magnetize them. We were all amused at the thought of the enemy pulling the metal poles up the rivers in a futile effort to clear their mines. As they say, all is fair in love and war.

One sidelight to the cruise happened to members of the ship's company. A new, slightly overweight Ensign (O-1), T.A. Winterstein, vowed to go on a strict diet to shed some pounds. As an incentive, he challenged a warrant officer (WO) to a contest to see who could lose the most weight during the cruise. (Red flag number one: warrant officers will outwit ensigns 99 percent of the time, so never get sucked into a wager with them.) At the weigh-in to establish the 'starting weight,' the agreement was signed and witnessed with $100 to be paid to the individual who has lost the most weight.

Ensign Winterstein was very self-disciplined through out the six month deployment, with a diet of salads, no bread or pasta, and no alcohol while in port. The WO, on the other hand, did not appear to change any of his eating habits. As the deployment finally finished, the day of reckoning came. Lo and behold, Ensign Winterstein had lost 22 pounds and was obviously pleased with his performance. His smile turned to a frown as the scale indicated a loss of 35 pounds for the WO. After the money changed hands and the bemused ensign returned to his quarters, it was revealed through the grape vine that the warrant had strapped metal bars to the inside of his legs at weigh-in, thereby increasing his weight by 40 pounds. I don't think Ensign Winterstein knows to this day that he was the victim of a scam.

One other significant event occurred that year. The ship had a CH-46 helicopter assigned so that all the ship's pilots could maintain their flight currency (and earn their flight pay) throughout their shipboard tour. While preparing for a maintenance flight while underway, I was flying in the right seat and I believe Major Busby was in the copilot's seat. The engines had started and the rotor blades were being held by the rotor brake when suddenly the rotors started turning. I looked over at the copilot, wondering why he had released the rotor brake prematurely. He replied, "I didn't touch anything." Just then a wall of fire dropped from the overhead and landed just aft and between the pilots' seats. I turned off the fuel switch on the console, released the rotor brake, and activated my emergency door lever. Meanwhile, the fire crew was approaching the aircraft but had to wait until the rotors came to a full stop. The aircraft was destroyed and could not be salvaged. I wasted no time departing the aircraft.

We later found out there was a computer malfunction that gave a 'full power' signal which overrode the rotor brake and the friction started the fire on the head. It was my first serious emergency in 14 years of flying and I wasn't even airborne.

The effects of the 'energy crisis', which was initiated in 1971 by Congress and President Nixon, who took us off the gold standard, resulted in inflation hitting 11 percent in 1974. The same year the Organization of Petroleum Exporting Countries (OPEC) sharply reduced the amount of oil exported abroad, causing gas shortages that resulted in long lines at gas stations. Real GDP fell 0.3 percent that year. Happy days were not forthcoming.

One memorable event occurred in September 1974 when a high

school friend of mine, Bucky DeVries, living near Hollywood, called me and asked if I would like to play in a celebrity tennis tournament for the benefit of Cedars-Sinai Hospital the following day. He was chairman of the celebrity committee, whose job it was to line up the elite of 'Tinsel Town.' Of course my answer was yes. It seems that Jonathan Winters had agreed to play, however when his wife found out he was scheduled to play on the same court as Edy Williams, a famous porn actress, she canceled Jonathan. The tournament had lined up a plethora of well-known stars such as Ed Ames, Desi Arnaz Jr., Edd Byrnes, Chad Everett, Farrah Fawcett, Monty Hall, Carl and Rob Reiner, Dan Rowan, Willie Shoemaker, Robert Stack, Dean Stockwell, Pat Studstill (all-pro end for Detroit), Alex Trebek, Dick Van Patten, and my partner, Edy Williams.

The only fact I knew about Edy was she was married to Russ Meyer, a producer of 'soft' porn films. What I didn't know was she had had 'encounters' with Richard Pryor in 1969, Reggie Jackson, Henry Kissinger, and George Jessel in 1973, Wilt Chamberlain in 1974 and was currently 'dating' Mickey Cohen. (all this while being married to Russ Meyer.) She was on the phone with her divorce lawyer between matches. By the way, she was a terrible tennis player and should have been playing in the novice division. Mickey Cohen, for those readers who do not follow stories of the underworld, was an LA gangster working for "Bugsy" Siegel and had established his credentials as an enforcer for Al Capone in Chicago. He was recently released from Federal penitentiary. After the last point was played (and we were crushed) Edy turned to me and said, "Here is my phone number. Call me if you ever get to LA again."

"Thanks," I replied, "but I have enough problems right now." I thought I had dodged a bullet, figuratively speaking. It was only much later that I realized I might have dodged one, literally.

On December 23, 1974 I flew my last flight from the deck of New Orleans and headed East to Patuxent River to complete my military career as the Navy's Chief Helicopter Test Pilot.

CHAPTER 13

Chief Helicopter Test Pilot

What every naval aviator aspires to happen in their career is to have a flying billet throughout every year of active duty.

ALTHOUGH I HAD not been passed over for the rank of captain, since my year group had not been in the promotion zone, the die was cast concerning my chances. Not only had I been evaluated 'seven of seven' by my air group commander, but had been graded 'three of three' in my final fitness report on the *New Orleans*. When the bad news finally arrived, I was strangely relieved. It meant I didn't have to face a tour in Washington at a non-flying desk job and could get on with the 'real world' experience of making a living as a civilian.

Meanwhile, I had a set of orders to serve as the Chief Helicopter Test Pilot at the Naval Air Test Center. Here was an opportunity to oversee the testing and evaluation of every new and improved helicopter and weapon system before it was sent to the fleet. In addition, I was serving with some of the best and brightest helicopter test pilots the Navy had to offer. What an opportunity!

Captain Bill Wirt was the Director of the Rotary Wing Aircraft Test Directorate and entered the navy as an enlisted aircrewman and later was commissioned as a fighter pilot. He began his helicopter career in 1950 (when I was a junior in high school) and had flown over 60 types of aircraft, including all the helicopters in the Navy inventory.

An 'old school' test pilot, he let me run the organization and only got involved with the day-to-day operations as necessary, which was ideal from my standpoint. Bill received the Navy Helicopter Association Bendix trophy for 'lifelong services' to vertical flight in 1978.

One of the more exciting endeavors during this tour was the evaluation of the Coast Guard's Short-Range Recovery (SRR) helicopter. Since the Coast Guard did not have an organization dedicated to testing aircraft, they requested NATC to evaluate the three candidate helicopters for the SRR mission. They were the S-76A, manufactured by Sikorsky Aircraft, the Bell 222, and the French Aerospatiale SA365C Dauphin. Three individual teams were formed with similar test plans to evaluate the three aircraft in those categories that permitted comparison. It was based primarily on observations during a single flight at all three sites in Texas, Connecticut, and France plus four days of ground evaluation. The observations were made by the Chief Test Pilot and Chief Engineer, Sea Control Branch, Rotary Wing.

A surprising revelation was observing French managers welcoming employees at the front door and thanking them for coming to work. Unbelievable to American managers, but maybe they are on to something. The defense industry in the U.S. has an annual resignation rate of seven percent. (Incidentally IBM Federal Systems averaged one resignation annually so they were obviously doing something right.) It was virtually impossible to fire French employees under the strict European Union rules.

Another surprising conclusion was that all three contenders met the general specifications of the mission. How were 'off-the-shelf' aircraft able to favorably compare, and in some cases outperform, helicopters that were designed from the hull up to meet a specific mission - and at a fraction of the cost? Could it be that the methodology for procuring military aircraft for the last 100 years was not as effective as letting manufacturers produce helicopters and buying them off their production line?

All three helicopters were given high marks for both meeting the specifications and being service suitable, the two categories on which all military aircraft are evaluated. In general, the aircraft weighed in between five and nine thousand pounds, delivered five to six hundred horsepower in each of two engines, flew about 165 knots with a range of 450 miles and had a ceiling of 19,000 feet. Their rate of climb varied from 1500 to 1750 feet per minute. Pretty impressive!

In the end, the Coast Guard selected the French Dauphin and thanked us for our efforts. We were happy to oblige.

A big change was occurring at NavAir regarding aircraft procurement. The airframe manufacturer was traditionally selected as the Systems Prime Contractor with the suppliers of avionics and all other aircraft equipment contracting through the Systems Prime. With the advent of the avionics playing such a major role in pursuing the anti-submarine and anti-ship missions, it was decided to designate the electronics systems designer as the Systems Prime Contractor. They would guarantee that performance specifications would be met with appropriate financial penalties if they failed. The Light Airborne Multipurpose System (LAMPS) led the way at NavAir in 1974 by choosing IBM Federal Systems as Systems Prime Contractor. Sikorsky Aircraft was none too pleased to be playing 'second fiddle' to a 'black box house.' It was felt by NavAir that successful development of this sophisticated weapons system by a non airframe contractor may cause a basic reappraisal of traditional procurement practices.

There were major complications in testing the LAMPS weapons system. With five SH-60B helicopters scheduled to be at the test center from 1980 through 1981, 10 dedicated pilots would be required, as well as six ASW equipment operators. The greater difficulty comes in the required increase in civilian test engineers and technicians, which peaked at 47 due to workload in 1981, then abruptly decreased by a factor of two only one year later. Despite the challenges, Rotary Wing Directorate felt confident of successfully evaluating one of the most promising ASW weapons systems in U.S. Navy history. I did not recognize at the time that IBM would play such a significant role in my future.

One of my test pilots was Ken Fugate, a captain in the Marine

Corps. Not only was he an accomplished helicopter pilot, but an outstanding tennis player. I grabbed him as a partner and successfully won the doubles title by defeating Wally Huggins and Allan Cox, 6-4, 6-4 in the finals of the anniversary tennis tournament at Devil's Reach Racquet Club in Woodbridge, Virginia. I must confess it was Ken's superior play that resulted in the title.

In other tennis news, I continued to participate in the celebrity tennis event in Los Angeles for several years at a cost of a $200 entrance fee plus purchasing an airline ticket. In 1977, I won the C+ doubles championship with a partner I picked up at the event, Joyce Grunauer. She developed stage fright so severe during the finals that I spent much of the match consoling her with encouraging words.

As the Navy's Chief Test Pilot, I felt an obligation to speak out about the high accident rate in the Navy as a whole and the helicopter community in particular. (Speaking truth to authority had already helped to terminate my career.) I penned an article for the Navy's safety magazine stressing we had to change our practices if we were to improve our record of one major accident every 15,000 flight hours. I pointed out that the Chief of Naval Operations, who sets the accident rate goals, was apparently satisfied with the loss of 112 aircraft, at an average cost of $21 million per major crash. It is interesting to note that pilot error is reportedly the dominant cause of accidents, followed by maintenance error and lastly, material failure. Aircraft design, as a cause factor, has always been sacrosanct, perhaps because aircraft are procured based on NavAir requirements and built to specification. To find design fault in operational aircraft would be to point an accusing finger at the highest levels of naval aircraft procurement, not an inviting assignment. I made the following points:

We have created a Safety Center, safety departments, safety committees, anonymous reporting programs, safety posters, safety magazines, safety stand-downs, and safety training schools. We have rewarded commands with no accidents and have relieved commanding officers with excessive numbers of accidents. There does not seem to be a panacea. Accidents continue. What do we have to lose with a change?

- Reduce the rapid turnover of personnel and supervisors. Everyone had just gotten there or is ready to leave.
- Operating conditions aboard ship are too often frantic. The task of getting on and off a pitching deck at night allows very little leeway for error. Slow down.
- Give higher priority to preserving assets, particularly in peacetime operations.
- If "Safety is paramount," as we proclaim, give the Safety Center the authority to ground aircraft for safety-of-flight reasons rather than the organization charged with 'fixing design flaws in the aircraft,' Naval Air Systems Command (NavAir).
- Design anti-FOD (foreign object damage) devices into aircraft engines.
- Treat each aircraft flight like an Apollo launch. Make safety the number one priority of commanding officers - not 100 percent availability, not launching marginal aircraft in marginal weather conditions, not air shows or fire-power demonstrations, and not accepting commitments that cannot be met by reasonable effort. Temper the can-do syndrome by recommending a 'no-to-the-boss' attitude.

The answer must be that if we do not improve, the Navy will run out of aircraft, Congress will run out of patience and conclude the country can no longer afford us.

The Safety Center published the article after revising the line about the CNO being satisfied with the loss of 112 aircraft (they changed it to a percentage) and deleted the recommendation that the Safety Center assume the authority to ground aircraft for safety reasons instead of NavAir. Change is hard for everyone and especially for an organization that has established traditions over many decades.

For a number of years, I have felt that young men should have some training in awkward social situations so I devised a four question completion quiz that I named The Gauche (gosh) Test. Gauche is a French word actually meaning left but has come to mean unsophisticated or socially awkward. Here are the four questions:

1. You are on a double-date with a brand-new partner sitting in the front seat with you. She accidently passes gas. You respond by saying _____.
2. Your date has had too much to drink during the evening and as you drop her off at her house, she throws up in the front seat. At her front door you say _____.
3. You are part of a group outing in a sleazy bar in Tijuana, Mexico with a floor show involving a young woman and a donkey. At intermission, one of your group invites the performer to your table and she sits next to you. You introduce yourself and say _____.
4. You are visiting a good friend and you have to make a rapid bathroom visit. You burst into the bathroom and find your friend's mother sitting on the throne. You say _____.

I was evaluating an H-46 helicopter with Ken Fugate operating out of Wilmington, Delaware International Airport so I was staying with friends in Doylestown, at the home of Lee and Clara Robinson. They had three children, Scott, Jeff, and Karen living at home and they had all taken the test and loved it. One evening a friend of Jeff, Chris Sands, who was on his wrestling team, was invited for dinner. They suggested that he take the test and Chris seemed anxious to do so. So, I gave him the first question.

His first answer was, "Wow, that really stinks."

The observers were quick to assist the visitor. "No, don't embarrass the poor girl. Say something like, excuse me. Pretend you made the mistake."

"OK, OK. What is the next question?"

With some reservation, I asked about the second situation with the sick date. He quickly responded, "Who's gonna clean up the car?"

The helpful kids, barely controlling their laughter, suggested holding her hand and telling her how sorry you were that she wasn't feeling well and that you would call her in the morning. By this time I foresaw that things were not going to improve so I proposed terminating the test.

"No, no" he insisted. "I get it now."

The conundrum about the girl in show business in Tijuana resulted in him answering," What a disgusting act you're involved in."

Immediate advice came from Scott. "She is humiliated enough. Change the subject. Ask her if she travels much."

With the training quiz a total failure, I pressed on to conclude the test. "What do you say to your friend's mother?"

He thought a moment and said, "Do you travel much?"

As I faced retirement from the Navy after 23 years of active service (plus 4 years at the Naval Academy), Rear Admiral John Wissler sent me a very nice farewell letter. One paragraph was particularly satisfying. "The responsibilities you accepted during this wide spectrum of duty assignments will serve you well in civilian life. The welfare of your men was foremost in your philosophy of leadership, and the re-enlistment figures earned during you squadron command attest to the wisdom of that style. Sound judgment and knowledge of your profession are your legacy, and the indelible impression of these qualities which you passed to the younger aviators will have a lasting effect."

An equally satisfying letter was one I received from a civil servant, Sam Cameron, with whom I had worked during several tours at NATC. One paragraph expressed his feeling quite well; "As a trainee in management science, I have learned a lot by watching you from the sidelines on such subjects as running meetings in a non-boring fashion, providing a broad perspective consult to Captain Wirt on several subjects that neatly hit the salient points of the issue, and pushing for the human side of the Navy. There is no way that George Washington University could include such nuances in their courses!"

To prepare for my entrance into the 'real world,' I signed up for a transition course at Drexel University and sent my résumé to an executive search firm to assist me in obtaining employment. At Drexel they give a battery of exams and had you fill out questionnaires on your preferences and desires. At the final interview with the director, he questioned why I had not done better academically at the Naval Academy?

I replied, "Because I wasn't as bright as many of my classmates."

"That is not factual. You tested at the level of my pre-med students," was his comeback.

With that, he recommended I pursue a livelihood in the world of non-profit organizations. I thanked him for his time and insight and set off to interview for jobs in the defense industry.

CHAPTER 14

The IBM Experience

Teamwork is essential; it allows you to blame someone else.

NOTHING TERRIFIES CAREER military officers more than being 'passed over' for promotion. The obvious reason is, of course, because the forced attrition methodology utilized in the armed forces allows younger officers into the 'pipeline' each year and forces the bottom half or third out on the street. A secondary and more subtle reason is that the military hierarchy reinforces the fear among career officers that 'life in the civilian sector is very competitive and there are not many companies that care about you as much as we do.' What if you can't find a suitable position in industry? Then what? Avoid this potential humiliation by remaining in the military for your 20 or 30 years. (Officers are permitted to remain in the service for a set number of years depending on the rank attained. If you become a major or lieutenant commander, you may remain for 20 years and retire at 50% of your base pay. A lieutenant colonel or commander is permitted to remain 26 years and a captain or colonel, 30 years with a 75% of base pay retirement.) The catch is that industry looks askance at anyone over the age of 45 unless they bring outstanding credentials or unusual qualifications to the table.

It is appropriate to outline the master plan for promotion in the Navy. It is based on the premise that a forced attrition system will eliminate poor performers fairly early in their career, which will benefit both the organization and the individual. (Actually, it wasn't designed to assist the individual officer at all, but early identification about one's potential to succeed in the military is an unintended consequence of the regulation.) So, in the 11th year or so, all lieutenants are brought before a promotion board to see which 75% are suitable to retain. Four years later, the records of all lieutenant commanders are presented to the board and 40% of them are culled out. Because of the competitive nature of the promotion system, anytime an individual officer receives even one 'average' fitness report, his career is probably limited. The problem with this system is that a professional disagreement with one's commanding officer or executive officer could be the curse of death. If promotion to next higher rank were a high priority in your military life, it would be prudent to save your 'silver bullet' objection for an extraordinary circumstance.

My initial introduction to IBM occurred in my role as Chief Test Pilot at Rotary Wing Directorate in the late 1970s. Naval Air Systems Command had done the unthinkable and selected an electronics company to be the prime contractor for a major weapon system; in this case, the Light Airborne Multi-Purpose System (LAMPS). Since I was finishing my active duty career of 23 years, my focus was to interview with various defense contractors and select the appropriate offer.

My first order of business was to sign up with a 'head hunter' to guide me through the job hunting process. I indicated that I did not want to be employed by Sikorsky Aircraft so they were to ignore them when sending out my résumé. Not only did they include Sikorsky in the mailing, they forwarded my notation that I had no desire to work for them. What a surprise when I learned they still wanted to interview me! Since my interviewing schedule included Kaman Aircraft, I thought it appropriate to include Sikorsky to share the expense, as I was driving up the East Coast to Connecticut.

The first words out of the hiring manager's mouth as I entered the office were, "Why don't you want to work for us?"

"Because your Chief Executive Officer lacks integrity," I quickly replied.

"We all know that," was the response. "We don't consider that a disqualifying reason to reject us."

After a short discussion, they wanted to keep the door open in case I changed my mind. I left the office thinking there seems to be a lot about industry employment that I didn't understand. Kaman ended up the only defense company that did not give me a job offer but I thanked them for the opportunity to interview with them. Virtually every interviewer, with the exception of IBM, asked how much my retirement pay amounted to. Several companies met my salary requirement of $30,000, but one offered $29,000. I immediately eliminated them from consideration. When I received an offer from IBM to start at $38,000, the search was over. I quickly accepted.

IBM Federal Systems Division, which employed about 5,000 people, was located in the village of Owego, New York, population 3700. The state of Pennsylvania is on the southern border and can be seen from Owego on a clear day. Incidentally, the number of sunny days that occur annually in the Southern Tier is among the lowest in the country. Skin cancer is almost unknown among its residents.

My history in changing assignments in the Navy was very different from what I experienced in industry. Career naval officers are rotated every two or three years during active duty. A move to a new location is not always viewed in a positive light since it usually involves selling and buying homes, relocating children in a new school and leaving old friends as you establish new ones at the assigned duty station. But, there are always old shipmates at the new locations to greet you and make you feel welcome. Such is often not the case in industry. I was not ready for the 'cold shoulder' I received when I reported to IBM for work in November 1979. As I showed up for work, I was greeted by my department manager, Tommy Payne, a 1966 Naval Academy graduate, with the words, "I don't want you in my department." Surprised, I retreated to my third-line manager, Peter Schultz, for a resolution. His solution was for me to join his staff for the time being. I later learned that Tommy's negative attitude toward hiring 'another helo pilot' was almost unanimous among the ex-Navy helicopter pilots working at IBM. I was mystified that seemingly rational employees could conclude that I was such an unwelcome threat when none of them had ever set eyes on me. Most of them eventually turned out to be good friends but it was not a smooth transition into civilian life.

My first 'duty station' was an off site assignment to the Naval Air Station at Patuxent River, Maryland to assist in the testing of the LAMPS helicopter. I was being paid per diem, on top of my normal salary, to live in my own house at 181 Gunston Drive, Lexington Park, MD. There were clearly decisions in the civilian world that I had to learn about in the years ahead.

The most significant event during this assignment was the break-up of my 24-year marriage to Donna. We had never been very compatible regarding our basic values and there was constant tension in the house over the years. I think that 10 deployments to the Western Pacific while I was in the Navy actually contributed to the longevity of the relationship. I finally realized that the only real solution to my personal unhappiness was to sever the cord of marriage. With three of the four children out of the house, I felt confident that the impact on the family would be minimal. I was glad to supply generous child support and lifetime alimony to Donna so she would not be financially impacted by the divorce.

As a member of Pete Schultz's staff at Patuxent River, I spent the majority of my time learning the business from the contractor's viewpoint and writing reports. Evidently, my writing ability impressed someone at the home office because I was assigned to the HH-60D Night Hawk helicopter proposal team upon my return to Owego. It was a big program ($56 million covering full-scale development) with a planned production of 243 Air Force helicopters to be used for Night Combat Rescue, a very challenging mission. The primary avionics to be incorporated were Night Vision Goggles, Infrared detectors, and Radar. As an aside, combat rescues during the Vietnam

War were a disaster; for every three downed airmen that we rescued, we lost two helicopters.

My specific responsibility was the section on Operational Effectiveness and I reported to Bill Sturm, the Program Director. Although I had never made a night combat rescue, my extensive knowledge of helicopter capabilities under instrument conditions, allowed me to convince the customer that our approach to mission success was viable. At the final walk-through, Bill was critical of my work and told me to change all the artwork in my book. When I asked for guidance, he suggested showing the mission avionics and indicating the function of each switch and button. Knowing that pilots would be reviewing this section, I could not believe my ears. I told Bill I would not do it. He immediately called my manager, Peter Schultz.

"Peter, this is Bill Sturm. One of your employees, Orv Wright, will not follow my directions on the HH-60D Proposal."

"Well, then fire him and send him home," Pete replied.

"I can't do that because no one else understands helicopter operations."

"Then, listen to him," Was Peter's final comment as he hung up.

The proposal was submitted as drafted and IBM Federal Systems was awarded the development contract. During the debriefing by the customer, Operational Effectiveness received the highest grade in the proposal and the Air Force representative commented, "It was obvious that you understood the mission and the key to making it a success. Well done."

The following year, the company gave Outstanding Achievement Awards to twelve employees on the proposal team, which included Bill Sturm and me. A cash bonus of $7,000 went along with the award. By this time, I was convinced that signing up with IBM was a wise decision.

Meanwhile, my love life took a holiday. Once the after-glow of a divorce wore off, the hard work of looking for a lifetime mate began in earnest. In short order I realized that all the marriageable women were either already married or in relationships. A time factor was involved. One had to wait until that 'ideal companion' was between relationships. Who knew dating was this complicated?

I had just spent New Year's Day 1983 in the Big Apple watching the ball drop with a beautiful ex-flight attendant and ex-wife of a helicopter pilot. She lived in Orlando and we had dated several times in 1982. Our last get-together was in her home town visiting Epcot in January and as we went our separate ways, she remarked, "Remember, we have no relationship." As I celebrated my 49th birthday that month, I began to question my goal of meeting my 'soul mate' before I got too old. I was hoping that it was darkest just before the dawn and 1983 would be a good year.

Lady Luck had not abandoned me. She had just taken a three year siesta. In March, Robin, the wife of Joe Harland, one of the helicopter pilots hired by IBM and a good friend, along with Meg Tillapaugh, introduced me to Carolyn Mullen, a native of Owego, NY. She was a home economics teacher and a recent divorcee. I invited her on a 'non-threatening' date to a movie followed by a midnight snack at Dennys. Although it was not love at first sight from her perspective (she asked if I wanted to date her sister), I knew she was the one. One year later we tied the knot and there is not a day that goes by that I do not thank my lucky stars to have married her and inherited her two children, Jenelle, 7, and Jeffrey, 3.

My next assignment, as manager of Heliport Operations Engineering, was one of my most satisfying positions at IBM. Not only was I the envy of all first-line managers because of my office with large windows overlooking the helipad, but possessing a very competent crew of Len Cohn (Operational Control Center and fueling), Walt Maginnis (Heliport Operations), Jerry Lesko (Control Tower), Sherm Parsons, John Force, and Walt Hawley (Flight Test Engineers) and our secretary, Tonya Green. In the first three years of operating, there was not a single accident or incident, either airborne or during ground operations.

Because conducting helicopter operations at an IBM plant was unusual, Federal Systems Headquarters in Bethesda, MD was quick to give Owego publicity through its quarterly business magazine. Here was a portion of one of the articles I was featured in, written shortly after the heliport opened. "The heliport was built specifically for helicopter avionics integration," says Orv Wright, manager of heliport operations. "The key word here is 'specifically.' While there are other heliports around the country, this is one of only two or three designed just for this purpose. It's not just another hangar..." Wright is responsible for all support required to test-fly helicopters on a pre-planned 60-mile triangular path above rolling hills and countryside. He continues: "The helicopters arrive from Sikorsky with IBM-provided minimum avionics, in this case 39 replaceable units that are just enough to navigate the aircraft. We then install what is called the mission avionics." The article goes on for another three or four pages with appropriate pictures. Very few first line managers got so well known so quickly at IBM.

IBM Federal Systems Owego was similar to a large, successful family. They expected employees to perform at a high level, were generous with compensation, and encouraged healthy extracurricular activities. In the autumn of 1983, the IBM Club awarded 144 trophies to winning participants in archery, golf, skeet and trap shooting, softball and tennis. I was lucky enough to win a trophy in tennis and it was presented to me by Joe Altobelli, manager of the World Champion Baltimore Orioles. This was just an example of the company's willingness to go 'first class.'

Following two managerial jobs in 1984 and 1985, I was having dinner with my wife at Taughannock Farms Inn, a fine-dining restaurant near Ithaca, when the IBM Owego General Manager (GM), George Houser, stopped by our table.

"Please stop by my office on Monday," George said. "I have a proposition for you."

Most first line managers, of which there were about 500 in Owego, had no relationship with the General Manager. But I had known George through the LAMPS program at Pax River. I had no idea why he wanted to see me. On Monday morning I showed up at his office and told his secretary that the GM wanted to see me. After a few minutes, George welcomed me and quickly got to the point.

"A major program, Combat Talon II, is in serious trouble; over budget and behind schedule. Our prime integrator, E-Systems, located in Greenville, Texas needs some tough love leadership, and I think you could fill the bill," George stated.

I sensed that this assignment would not be highlighted in my obituary, but I saluted and told the family we were off to Texas for a two year assignment at E-Systems. I am unsure whether I could have improved the performance of E-Systems, even if I had been given the authority to institute changes (which I was not given), but it was an interesting experience and helpful for future assignments. I was promoted to Senior Engineer/Manager while off-site, so time spent in Texas had some upside. Carolyn took advantage of her free time and upgraded her teaching credentials through courses at East Texas State University. She was now qualified to teach Math and Science. The children learned all about Texas history in elementary school, but we all agreed that there are better places to raise teenagers than the Lone Star State.

The first month at E-Systems was spent renting a house, getting the children registered for school, finding local doctors and all the one hundred and one required tasks when relocating. With two children in elementary school, we thought it prudent to join the local country club since it had a pool. (Texas is really hot in the summer.) The manager was very accommodating and insisted he would like to meet my wife and welcome her to the neighborhood. After introductions, we paid our annual dues and were declared active members. It wasn't until later that a local resident informed me that the manager wanted assurance I was not married to an African-American. With no experience with Southern attitudes, the revelation came as a complete surprise.

At the time, I was unaware of the Lenell Geter fiasco. Lenell was a black mechanical engineer, hired by E-Systems in 1982 following his graduation from South Carolina State in June 1981. In August there were a series of armed robberies in the Dallas area and Lenell was identified by five eye-witnesses as the perpetrator. Despite eight co-workers, including his manager, testifying that Lenell was at work that day and not robbing a Kentucky Fried Chicken restaurant in Balch Springs (50 miles from Greenville), an all-white jury in October found him guilty and the judge sentenced him to life in prison. Fortunately, the NAACP and Sixty Minutes took up his case and he was released in December 1983 and given a new trial. In March 1984, the actual criminal was captured and confessed and all charges against Lenell were dropped. I relay this incident to show the culture of Greenville, Texas in the mid-1980s.

The decade of the 80s was also significant in the original Wright family with all four children getting married. It started in the summer of 1982 with Steve tying the knot with Noriko, a Japanese national, in New York City. I must confess not all family members thought it would last a lifetime, but, we were all wrong. They created and raised three boys and she was the perfect wife for Steve for 34 years, dying prematurely in 2016. Doug was next, marrying Denise Morrissette, a Navy junior, in 1984. Although they were high school sweethearts and produced a smart and athletic girl, the relationship ended after 10 years. John married next in 1989, teaming up with Jagi Lamplighter, a classmate at Saint Johns College in Annapolis, Maryland. They are still going strong after producing three boys and adopting a 14 year-old-girl from China. Last to join the club was Nanette in the early 90s when she went international and found her 'one and only' Adam Davidson from Sydney, Australia. At their 'Camelot-like' wedding dinner at a national park in St. Mary's County, I gave the traditional 'Father of the bride's' speech, wearing my dress blue uniform, minus the ceremonial sword.

"When my children were 12, 10, 8, and 4-years-old respectively, I asked each of them what would be the most flattering comment they could ever receive." Steve responded with, "If someone stated that he, (Steve) was the smartest person they had ever met." Doug said, "If someone described me as the nicest boy they knew." John thought it would be most flattering if someone said, "I love you." And Nanette finished the conversation by exclaiming that she would be most pleased if someone asked, "Will you marry me?" I then looked over at Adam and said, "Thank you Adam, for making a 4-year-old girl's dream come true." As I sat down, I was confident that she had made the right choice and they would live happily ever after. (Not all of my predictions about interpersonal relationships have come true.)

As 1987 drew to a close, and upon returning to Owego from E-Systems in Texas, I was appointed as the manager of Field Engineering with sites in the Philippines, Germany, and Italy. It brought its own unique situations to solve since one of our employees in Sicily was fire-bombed and some government employees working in the Philippines travel office were burglarizing the residents who were transferring out. After two years, the manager of Integrated Logistics Support (ILS), Jack Underwood, offered me a second-level manager's position in his 100 person strong organization. Logistics is the management of the flow of things between their point of origin and their final destination. It involved supervising four first line managers who were responsible for Systems Engineering, Combat Talon II Logistics Engineering, Maintainability, and Avionics Systems Engineering and Training. The assigned managers were all dedicated and competent engineers; Gerard Corprew, Roger Vick, Ron Young, and Pat Nally. Although logistics was certainly not my area of expertise, I felt pleased that Jack had recognized that I possessed the required managerial skills to succeed in the position. For the next four years I lived in the world of logistics and did my best to encourage all employees to strive to improve their reputation as professionals in their field.

To maintain fitness and pursue my love for tennis, I started to play competitively at the 3.5 level (similar in skill level to a Division III college player). Here are excerpts from the local Binghamton newspaper; "Orville Wright and Diane Vajay won a 7-5 third-set tiebreaker victory over a pair from New York City that gave the Oakdale Racquet Club team a victory in the Eastern Tennis Association mixed doubles championship at SUNY-Albany. The three-day tournament had teams from five regions; New York City, Long Island, Northern, Southern and Western New York, which was represented by the Oakdale Racquet team. With the win, the Oakdale team will play in the Northern Atlantic Mixed Doubles Tournament in two weeks in New Haven, Conn. Oakdale, pushed to three sets nine times in 12 matches, defeated each region by 2-1 scores. Had Wright and Vajay not won, the Northern team would have been declared the winner," according to Ron Yanko, who won all four matches he was involved with. Northern had won more matches than we did so that one was critical."

From a professional development standpoint, I joined the American Institute of Aeronautics and Astronautics (AIAA) in the early 1980s and by May 1986 was appointed Chairman of the AIAA Technical Committee on Flight Testing. This was significant since it meant I was following in the footsteps of one of the all-time legends in the world of flight testing, Scott Crossfield, who was the first Chairman.

In my last year in the ILS organization, I received a Management Award, which 'recognizes success in achieving all business measurements while maintaining a positive balance of human resource management skills and objectives.'

In many of my chapters, I have expressed my leadership techniques and beliefs to the reader, but third party views carry much more weight since self-imposed bias (and ego) is eliminated. I received a letter from one of my ILS managers, Mike Elsner, several years after transferring from the organization.

"As one goes through life, you don't always fully appreciate that what you have until it is gone. To that end, I just want to take a minute and thank you for providing the adult leadership for ILS during your tenure here. Even though I know I was very lucky to have worked under your leadership, I'm not sure I ever said thank you for all the honest advice and council you provided me. You never told me what to do. You led me to conclusions and guided me in decisions, never commanding or ordering. I always felt I could confide in you without reprisal. Thank you for all your help, trust, and faith in me as a manager and person." Signed, Mike

Even though my primary assignment during these years was in the ILS organization, I was called upon to be a member of the proposal team for the EH-101 Helicopter Program to be developed for the Royal Navy, competing against British Aerospace Corporation and GEC Avionics. We were teamed with Westland Helicopters in the UK, and Agusta, located in Italy. It was considered such a 'must-win' program that both assistant General Managers, Galen Ho and Ed Gormley participated in the proposal preparation. We were successful at winning the largest contract in the history of the IBM Corporation. Many employees on the proposal team were given monetary awards including me. An 'elite' team of specialists was assembled and plans were generated to guarantee all specifications promised to the Royal Navy would be met in a timely manner. Those working on the program would reside in the UK for three years with an option to extend for certain key individuals. The compensation package given to team members was quite generous although uprooting family members was challenging in many cases. Although the vast majority of the team started their assignment in the early 90s, I was scheduled to make the move three or four years later since I would be involved in the flight test portion of the program.

CHAPTER 15

Oh, To Be In England

*If God had meant for us to travel tourist class,
he would have made us a lot narrower.*

THE UNITED KINGDOM (UK) is made up of four countries (England, Scotland, Wales, and Northern Ireland). It is the size of Oregon with a population of about 94 million subjects.

Early in 1990, Harris Belman, a marketing executive from IBM Federal Systems Owego, learned about a new contract that was about to be let by the British Ministry of Defence (MOD) to act as System Prime Contractor for the delivery of 44 anti-submarine warfare (ASW) helicopters. Only contractors with 'deep pockets' were permitted to bid since the penalties for failure to meet performance guarantees were severe and could bankrupt smaller companies. Having convinced the top-level financial planners at headquarters that this multi-billion dollar contract made economic as well as political sense, the Owego proposal team set about preparing the humongous technical and cost bid. I was invited to participate as the operational book manager based on my track record on a similar Air Force proposal and the fact that the proposal team's first choice was unavailable.

IBM immediately teamed with Westland Helicopter Limited to compete against British Aerospace, the largest defense company in the UK. We had one leg up in that we were teamed with the British helicopter manufacturer from which the MOD was planning to procure the basic EH-101 airframe. In addition, the MOD was unimpressed with European contractors' reluctance to guarantee their work. On the downside, we were an American company and there was no shortage of British subjects that remembered 1776 with unforgiving fervor.

After many months of collecting data in the UK, we proceeded with a campaign of intense writing, editing, rewriting, and converting the proposal to 'Brit-Speak.' The next few months were spent interpreting the tome to the MOD representatives. Whether it was the compelling documentation, the insightful oral presentations or the disenchantment with the appalling record of British defense contractors (they all insisted on cost plus contracts with no guarantees), the MOD never made clear, but Owego was awarded the largest contract (three billion dollars) in IBM's history. There was much jubilation when the announcement came, with almost no thought as to how we were going to live up to all those promises we so glibly put forward in our proposal.

In our haste to position the 200-strong expatriate team of engineers and administrators in the UK, we failed to realize a three year commitment was totally inadequate for a 10 year program. Not only would the helicopters be just phasing into the test program at the end of three years, but we also did not have the resources available to staff a relief team that was close to comparable with the very capable 'first team.' A second misjudgment was similar to that made by Admiral Hyman Rickover when he established such high standards for selection to the nuclear submarine fleet in the early 1960s. He had his choice of officers from over 50 conventionally-powered submarines to staff 10 nuclear boats. The Admiral was a bully with a huge ego and since his judgment was 'divinely inspired,' his non selection of diesel submarine officers was final. That was all well and good until the entire submarine fleet was soon converted to nuclear and this whole band of seasoned, experienced officers had been eliminated from further consideration. The result was a series of military policies that progressively lowered the standards for submarine officers starting with suspension of the requirement to be a surface ship Officer Of the Deck (OOD) prior to submarine training, and ending with 'drafting' new college graduates into nuclear submarine training. IBM's consequence was not as significant since we only judged a few candidates 'not sufficiently talented' to make the initial Merlin team. Unfortunately, the list of qualified replacement engineers willing to sign on for a three or four year tour of duty in England was very short indeed.

The company was quite generous with their initial compensation package. Employees would receive liberal cost of living allowances in addition to company-funded annual vacations to the United States as well as payment of English taxes including local Council taxes (similar to our school and county taxes). They would also transfer house pets, assist in selling your car, give an allowance to purchase an auto in the UK, pay for driving lessons, and even pay an equivalent amount for your house payment in the US (even if your house was paid for). You can see why the package was characterized as generous.

The Merlin team got off to a good start and made a favorable impression on the customer with its enthusiasm, knowledge, and work ethic. The expatriates, who came primarily from Owego, but also from Manassas and other IBM sites around the country, had some difficulty integrating with the non-Owego IBM members on the program. Integrating with the Westland team members was a higher hurdle to maneuver. Issues that surfaced almost immediately were:

- The basic workweek. The British employees were paid for a 37 hour workweek. The U.S. employees were paid for 40 hours, expected to work between 50 and 60, and received one hour of compensatory time off for every eight hours of overtime worked. The Brits were given a pay raise for a full 40 hour week.
- Parking. The British felt individual engineers should have assigned parking spaces so they wouldn't have so far to walk to

get to work in the morning. The Americans took the position that if you wanted a parking spot close to the door, you just showed up at an earlier hour.

- Holiday Plans. To the British, a planned holiday (vacation in Brit-speak) was sacrosanct. No business crisis would ever be severe enough to have an employee postpone his holiday for the company. We were accustomed to modifying personal plans when they conflicted with important business endeavors. The British culture allowing holiday plans to take precedence was accepted.
- Language barriers. Some words have completely different meanings depending on which side of the Atlantic you reside. To 'table' a topic in America means to defer discussion until a later time. In Britain, it means addressing it immediately.
- Besides learning to drive on the left side of the road, Americans were accustomed to driving with a 'miss distance' of eight feet from oncoming traffic on a two lane road. In England, the narrower roads allowed a 'miss distance' of only four feet. Blown out tires on the left side of the car, when hitting the curb, resulted.
- In the first three years of the program, American team members, driving on the 'wrong' side of the road, had totaled six or seven rental cars from Hertz. Hertz had a preprinted accident form entitled, 'IBM Accident Form.'

Transportation

Change is hard for most people. It is doubly hard when introduced to a new culture. I will use transportation as an example of what we expatriates experienced during our assignment. The British love their cars. They also live on a small island with a finite number of roads as well as a government policy that banned all future road building. To complicate the formula, about 700,000 new cars are registered each year. In order to cope with this dilemma, a government policy was instituted to levy a gas tax of 6 percent above inflation to encourage car owners to give up driving, and take public transportation instead. From 1997 to 2000, the cost of a gallon of gas (petrol) went from $3.64 to $5.20. The weekly budget for an average UK household was: Transportation - $108; Housing - $102; Food - $101. Car insurance increased 50 percent in the five years I lived in the UK, despite the fact that British drivers had the lowest accident rate in the world. Driving instruction was necessary, if you want to pass the driving test (which they grade on a curve with only 56 percent passing on the first try) at a cost of $31 an hour for 12 lessons. The road test is $61 unless you want it on a Saturday, and then it is $75.

Health Care

Most Americans are aware that the UK has a National Health Service (NHS) and it is often used as an example when lobbying for a similar system such as 'Medicare for All.' NHS was initiated right after World War II when the Labour government under Clement Atlee regained political power from the Conservative Party under Winston Churchill. It was designed to ensure that all subjects would have access to health care regardless of ability to pay. Here are some end-of-20th century facts about the NHS:

- At $100 billion a year, it consumes 20 percent of the entire UK budget.
- Prescriptions are 'free' if you are at least 60 years-old. As expatriates, our older team members and their dependants were eligible.
- Because doctors and nurses are civil servants and are paid an annual salary, there is a serious shortage of medical professionals. From 1990 until 1997, NHS lost 50,000 nurses due to low pay.
- Making an appointment to see a General Practitioner was quick and responsive; however, wait times to see a specialist were excessive. The number of patients waiting over 13 weeks was 485,000. The number waiting over 26 weeks was

146,000. These were the statistics in the late 1990's and may no longer be valid.

- After seeing a specialist, if an operation is recommended, there is another delay before that event takes place. A cataract removal averaged 150 days. A hip replacement took 180 days. Private insurance patients went to the head of the queue.

Other British practices that surprised our team members were: Every owner of a TV set was charged an annual tax of $160. (No charge if you were over 70.) Welfare and government pensions (equivalent to our social security) consumed 30 percent of the entire budget at $160 billion. Their defense budget is a miniscule $30 billion. At 137,000 members-strong, nearly the entire British Army, Navy, and Air Force could fit in London's Wembly Stadium. (The U. S. has ten times that number.)

After several years, the company realized it would be prudent to cut back on their compensation package to the newly assigned expatriates. I was one of the first to experience the downgrade. It was so severe that it would have cost me a reduction in pay of $50,000 to take the assignment. (Thirty thousand of those dollars from eliminating my wife's teaching salary.) When I balked at the loss in pay, I was told to accept the package or turn down the assignment. I chose the latter and informed my projected manager in the UK, Joe Harland, of the situation. Joe immediately informed his boss, Galen Ho, that I could not take the assignment under those conditions. Galen directed Joe to find a replacement. After two weeks of searching, Joe reported that he was unable to find a qualified substitute. Galen's response was, "Then pay him the same as everyone else."

The EH-101 (Merlin) team was divided into two distinct locations under the leadership of Peter Schultz. The vast majority of the team was located at Her Majesty's Portsmouth Naval base, home of two-thirds of the Royal Navy's surface ships. A small contingent was assigned to Westland Helicopter Company in Yeovil, England. The Yeovil group consisted of three departments, Integration (managed by Laurie Holdridge), Qualification (managed by Martin Jeffries, a British engineer), and Flight Test, managed by me. We all reported to Joe Harland, Technical Director, in Portsmouth.

The American test team varied in size over the five years I was there but there were some of the 'elite' members who planned and conducted the required testing of the Merlin Weapon System: Darrell Murray (his wife managed the Integration department), Roger Vick (recruited from the ILS department), Rich Matias (wife Jeanne worked for Integration), and Nick Babey (married Paula, a UK resident). They were all highly dedicated 'self-starters' that needed virtually no managing. Our contract secretary, Karen McKenzie, was worth her weight in gold, guiding all the Americans in the way of the British, arranging parties, insuring all hands knew of all the required meetings and acting as a 'mother hen,' when required. Her efficiency created a positive professional reputation for the entire department.

The EH-101 Merlin helicopter itself was quite impressive. With an empty weight of 23,000 pounds and a crew of three (pilot, observer, and crewman), it could lift 9,000 pounds of ordnance, cargo, combat troops, or a combination. It was powered by three Rolls Royce Turbomeca RTM 322 engines, generating 2100 horse power each. Its top speed was 167 knots and had a range of 450 nautical miles. It could stay airborne for five hours and was designed to operate from Type 22 Royal Navy frigates in seas with wave heights exceeding 12 feet and winds up to 55 miles per hour. It could lose one engine in a hover at maximum gross weight and safely fly away. The avionics package was very sophisticated with a four-axis autopilot, automatic stabilization system, GPS, obstacle warning system, TACAN (Tactical Air Navigation system that gives bearing and distance from a transmitter), a digital automatic flight control system and a network of helicopter management and mission systems designed to reduce pilot workload. The package was necessary since we were establishing single pilot capability for a nighttime, ASW mission that had required two pilots in the past.

Although the program had lost one of it's preproduction (PP) test aircraft in 1993 in Italy (which resulted in a temporary flight delay of six months), we were accident-free at Westland until April 7, 1995. A general rule among military helicopter operators is to require parachutes only on flights scheduled to exceed 3,000 feet above ground level. The test on this calamitous day was to be conducted at 10,000 feet altitude in the 4th preproduction helicopter (PP-4), so all four airmen were wearing parachutes. The Merlin helicopter was designed with a long fuselage and flew with a slight 'nose up' attitude in a hover, so the size and strength of the tail rotor shaft met the minimum safe limits, but just barely. Just minutes after establishing test altitude, there was a loud 'bang,' followed by a rapid clockwise rotation of the aircraft. Both crewmen in the cabin wasted no time in departing the crippled helicopter and activated their chutes when clear of the descending craft. (I later interviewed one of the crewmen and asked him how hard his decision to bail out was. He quickly stated, "Easiest decision I have ever made, despite never having jumped out of a plane before.") The co-pilot left the cockpit from the left seat about 5,000 feet and the pilot in command did not depart until about 1,000 feet when it was obvious he was unable to regain control. As the pilot bailed out, his parachute snagged on one of the aircraft's protrusions, but he managed to free himself just seconds before the helicopter crashed. The only injury was a compression fracture of the spinal cord of the pilot, who regained flight status about six months later. PP-4 was a total loss! The accident investigation confirmed that the tail rotor had failed due to a stress fracture.

The contract called for the delivery of 44 production Merlin helicopters to the Royal Navy (RN), but it was to be done in stages. The MOD ordered 22 production helicopters in early 1995 and Italy purchased 16 more later that year. The first Merlin was delivered to the RN in May of 1997, even though the testing verification was not scheduled for completion at the Atlantic Undersea Test and Evaluation Center (AUTEC) in the Bahamas until 1999 and 2000. All 44 aircraft were delivered to the UK by December 2002. Even though not all the countless specifications were met (a virtual impossibility), some financial penalties were assessed and other specifications were waived. All in all, the customer was very pleased with the performance and the service suitability of the Merlin Weapons System. The helicopter was subsequently purchased by Denmark, Portugal, Japan, and India.

Several years after IBM Federal Systems contracted with the MOD for the 44 Merlins, the company was sold to Loral Corporation in 1994, who in turn, sold it in 1996 to Lockheed Martin Corporation for $9 billion. (The same year, Loral was accused of transferring space technology to China and paid a fine of $20 million.) The sale was meaningless to the Merlin team since all the managers and employees remained the same.

A variant of the EH-101, the VH-71 Kestral, was selected to be the follow-on helicopter for the U.S. Presidential transport fleet. However, the program was cancelled due to cost overruns in 2007 when then Senator John McCain criticized President Obama for wanting such an expensive means of transportation. The cancellation cost the taxpayers over one billion dollars in termination fees and sunk costs (preproduction aircraft already paid for) of the program. The taxpayers received absolutely nothing in return. This terrible political decision was largely ignored by the press. The aging fleet of H-3 Presidential helicopters had to be replaced several years later.

When I arrived in the UK in early 1995, the British economy was growing at two percent a year; inflation was two point five percent with an unemployment rate of five percent. There was a non competitive culture in Britain, which accepted the fact that 95% of all groceries were sold by just four companies. Any piece of electronic equipment was priced within one pence throughout the country. In the U.S. we would call that price fixing, but they called it a 'nice profit margin.' The grocery stores in the UK averaged a profit margin of eight percent compared to about one percent margins in the USA. Housing prices in the UK were increasing at 20% a year, which suggested it would be wise to purchase a house rather than rent for the three or four years we were planning to reside there. It proved to be a smart decision since we later sold our brick, four bedroom, two bathroom house with a two car garage at 97 Southway Drive in Yeovil for $40,000 more than we paid for it. I had to make the search, and purchase it on my own since Carolyn and Jeffrey were not scheduled to arrive until summer. It was not a decision I would recommend for the average husband, but in this case, it worked out.

Roger Vick, a friend from Owego, had purchased a house and invited me to reside there until my family could join me in June. He had just gotten married and was waiting for his native Californian wife, Connie, to make the flight over. When she arrived in March, Roger suggested I could continue to occupy one of their bedrooms for the time being. Carolyn strongly suggested that I move out immediately since it was not appropriate to interfere with the daily living schedule of 'newly-weds.' When Connie appeared, she encouraged me to stay on so I lived rent free for a few more months.

I decided to write a company confidential quarterly report for our employees, as well as those remaining behind in Owego. It consisted of sections about Local Happenings, Company Connections, Around the Globe, Opinions & Speculation, and PotPourri. It was typically 14 or 15 pages long and soon had a large following in the Owego Plant. The Communications Department got their hands on a copy and sent me a 'cease and desist' letter, stating I had no authority to generate any company-related information. I objected and contacted the General Manager with a copy of my latest report. He decided that I should continue with a small adjustment by labeling it 'proprietary.' Here is a typical story under Opinions;

- Based upon actual risk, where are you most likely to die?
  a) Driving in the USA   b) Flying on an African Airline
  c) Playing rugby in the UK   d) Being hospitalized with a non-life threatening disease.
  Although one should avoid both b) and c), over 40,000 people lose their lives annually driving on U.S. highways. Between 44,000 and 98,000 patients entered U.S. hospitals last year with relatively minor problems and failed to survive the ordeal.

The work in the UK was demanding and long hours were required but there was still a lot of time for socializing. Once a week, many of the employees in Yeovil gathered at a pretty country pub, The Lamb Inn, in Tintinhull. It was located on the outskirts of Yeovil and was the perfect venue for an evening of social tennis followed by a delicious dinner. Laurie Holdridge and I joined the Yeovil Tennis Club and played competitive club tennis for several years. As I think back, we lost very few matches. A side benefit of belonging to the local tennis club was having access to tickets for the Wimbledon Championships each year, a memorable event for our entire family.

Another benefit that virtually every Merlin team member took advantage of was the ability to travel to European and Asian countries over the factory shutdowns for the Christmas and New Year holidays. Here are a list of countries we visited during our five-year adventure and my short observations:

- Egypt – One of the most fascinating countries we visited. The trip to view the Pyramids and the giant Sphinx was almost surreal. Three million tourists made the journey annually in the late 90s. Tourism has fallen off dramatically due to fear of terrorism.
- India – The Taj Mahal located in Agra was impressive but it could be improved by a periodic cleaning. Also, an observed body floating down the Ganges River was a turnoff. Poverty in India was indescribable but, as I was observing traffic in Delhi, I saw a camel pulling a cart followed by a Rolls Royce and then an elephant with a rider accepting money from bystanders. Simply unbelievable!
- Spain – We spent a week there visiting my cousin, who makes a living as a military arms saleswoman. Spain is an impressive and beautiful country with weather that is the envy of most New Yorkers.
- Italy – Another beautiful European country with so many historical sites that a tourist will never have enough time to see

them all. Florence is quite impressive and the Leaning Tower of Pisa is a 'shouldn't miss' destination.

- France – It has been said that the French do not deserve to live in such a wonderful country. Paris is magical and the south of France is just as magnificent. One can understand why so many Americans in the 1930s became expatriates.

- Iceland – A one day trip to this unusual country was eye opening. Most residents have only one name and fish is the primary food consumed. They actually believe in fairies and there were no trees on the island. Hot water was piped into one's house directly from hot springs; no hot water heaters.

- Norway – Another one day trip exposed us to impressive fiords and beautiful inlets. The residents are attractive and athletic-looking. A one day view of a country of this size is certainly not comprehensive. Most of our time was spent on a small ship.

- Estonia – Spent a long weekend in the capital city of Tallinn. The country was violently anti-Russian, having just had their independence restored in 1991. Restaurants were very inexpensive and several team members spent a memorable evening in an Estonian pub in a sing along while Connie Vick (wife of Roger) displayed her marvelous talent on the piano playing show tunes.

- Ireland – Perhaps the most beautiful country in Europe. Spent a week touring and watched in awe as sheep dogs put on an impressive show. The Irish were very welcoming and warm.

- Belgium – A small country between France and Holland, about the size of Maryland. A trip to Bruges, with its picturesque bridges, is worth the effort. It is also a beer lovers dream, with numerous breweries.

- Germany – Spent some time in Munich during their annual beer festival. Big mistake. So many people we were almost crushed to death. Of all the European countries, Germans were most like Americans in their personalities and behavior.

My good friends, Roger and Connie Vick departed the UK several months before my retirement and I had the opportunity to organize, and be Master of Ceremonies for their 'going away' party that was held at a local English pub. All of Roger and Connie's British friends attended as well as virtually all the American team members. It turned into an amiable 'roast' with a lot of laughs and memorable moments highlighted. I received a very nice compliment from one of the English attendees when he said, "You have only been in our country for five years, yet you picked up our sense of humor already." I just nodded in agreement and smiled.

The five-year assignment finally ended in September 2000 and, as a 'retirement gift,' the MOD approved a flight for me in a preproduction Merlin EH-101. They allowed me to takeoff, fly during the test mission, and land at the field upon return. It was an exhilarating experience and one I shall never forget. There is no way that an American Department of Defense official would have allowed me to fly their $21 million aircraft.

The final coup de grace was our trip back to the U.S. on the Queen Elizabeth II. It gave us five days to decompress after five stressful and bountiful years.

CHAPTER 16

Retirement

It is better to retire too soon than too late.

RETIREMENT! THE WORD has as many meanings to people as the word marriage. To some it is Nirvana; the payoff for 40 years of struggle. To others it symbolizes an opportunity for self directed interests. A third group views it as loss of camaraderie and social intercourse. A small but significant number regret the loss of status and the joy of working. Still others find the reduction in financial compensation painful since it brings a lower quality of life. It is strange that very few people are truly ready for the change in lifestyle that this inevitable stage brings. Like interpersonal relationships, everyone must figure it out for themselves.

My plan was to work in industry for 20 years and retire in 1999 with a pension from IBM to supplement my Navy stipend. The purchase of the Federal Systems arm of IBM by Loral (and subsequent sale to Lockheed Martin) altered the plan somewhat. As it turned out, IBM allowed anyone over 55 years of age with 15 years of employment to retire with an immediate pension. This meant that I would continue to work at the same salary in the same job while receiving a 'windfall' for being an 'old' employee. What a deal! It meant that the monthly retirement check from IBM could be used to fund Jenelle's and Jeff's college education with no impact on our daily cost of living. As my planned retirement date approached, I was asked to extend one year in England to finish the flight testing of the Merlin EH-101 helicopter. I accepted the request and set September 1, 2000 as my official 'end of working' life.

When the first day of September rolled around, I was in the middle of the Atlantic Ocean on the Queen Elizabeth II with my wife, Carolyn, dressed in formal clothes and savoring the trip home. It was appropriate to make the transition from worker to 'free-loader' last longer than a seven-hour plane ride in the back of a U.S. Airways commercial aircraft. After years on U.S. Navy ships, it was so pleasant being a passenger on the famed QE 2. The theme for the crossing was British authors. One author, in particular, made an anguished plea to write your memoirs, if you were at all capable of attempting it. I took it under advisement and put it on the 'back shelf.' I had also arranged for a limousine to meet us in New York and deliver us to Owego to extend the fantasy several more hours.

There is no shortage of experts regarding the subject of retirement. The overwhelming focus in advice columns is how to prepare financially since one may be dependent on savings and investments for 30 or 40 years. They all advise to start early and give up daily lattes and invest those three dollars in equities. No one ever takes the advice, which is why so many people face retirement with a reduced quality of life and hoping they will someday win the lottery. With four pensions and two social security checks between us, financial concerns were last on our list of challenges.

There are a number of differences between taking a two-week vacation from your job and leaving work for the last time. After the initial realization that you now control your agenda, you think, in no particular order, what the future holds and what worlds are left to conquer. Here was part of my 'to do' list:

- Maintain fitness and a healthy lifestyle. I was hoping to do this playing tennis.
- Learn to play the piano. This was a necessary step to complete my next task.

- Perform a one-man musical comedy show with satirical songs.
- Ensure my children did not end up living in poverty during their retirement.
- Find a meaningful way to contribute to society or at least to my community.
- Write a book.

The idea to maintain fitness is an almost universal resolution. Examine the gym memberships that explode in January of each year. By March, the required self discipline has disappeared with the same rationalization as the diet promise. 'For sure next year, we'll hit it hard' is the lament after continuing failures. The facts show that Americans, on average, gain one pound a year for every year after 30 years of age. Very few can fit into the tuxedoes or wedding dresses they got married in. I have been fortunate to have participated in sporting activities my entire life. Whether it's playing basketball into my late 40s or playing tennis most of my life, fitness came as a welcome byproduct and not something that I had to concentrate on. Having been introduced to Pickle Ball by Laurie Holdridge, a tennis friend, I play two or three times a week at the local Boys and Girls Club in Owego or Endicott. It is a fast game played with a whiffle ball and an oversized ping pong paddle on a shortened tennis court with a net similar to tennis. It is very popular among senior citizens, especially in Florida. The annual New York Empire games bring Pickle Ball teams from all over the state to play in age-related competition. I entered with another octogenarian, C.K. Lim, and won gold medals two years in a row.

In retirement, I started playing United States Tennis Association (USTA) competitive tennis at the 3.5 level. After several years playing for a Binghamton team, my Owego friends pressured me to 'jump ship' and join them, which I subsequently did. We had a very successful run that ended up with my team defeating both Buffalo and Rochester and playing in the USTA Nationals playoff in Arizona. Although we only finished 9th out of 15 teams, my partner, Dale Wise, and I won 3 out of our 4 matches. It was due to Dale's superior play, not mine. The next two years, most of our team members were up-graded to 4.0 and we were not up to the challenge. The competition was too good.

Maintaining a healthy lifestyle is quite different from avoiding health-related issues. In 2003, following an annual physical examination, I was diagnosed with early stages of prostate cancer. My decision to undergo eight weeks of radiation treatment allowed me to continue my normal daily activities with no side effects. The complete elimination of the disease is a testament to modern medicine.

A second health issue struck several years later, after I experienced knee pain walking for a short distance. I attributed it to an old football injury I suffered in high school in 1950. The medical staff insisted on complete X-rays, which showed deterioration of the right hip and a recommendation of a hip replacement. The operation itself was relatively pain-free and the eight-week rehab was successful, but it definitely had a deleterious effect on my tennis game. I went from a 3.5 to a 3.0 and gave up playing in USTA competition. I still play social tennis twice a week but I have to rely on the skill of my partners to come out on top. I have gotten used to saying, "yours."

I used to watch satirist Mark Russell on PBS playing piano and using humor to highlight political themes and other current events. Although he was an adequate piano player, I didn't think his humor or satire was particularly entertaining and I thought, 'I can do that, and probably better.' My first problem to solve was how to play the piano. I purchased a second-hand piano and had a neighbor, Mike Mansfield, tune it. In the process, he inquired who was going to play the instrument. When I told him my plan to do a one-man comedy show using the piano, he replied, "You are the least funny person I know." With that ringing endorsement, I looked into hiring a piano teacher.

Carolyn recommended a long-time acquaintance, Jane Erickson, whom I contacted and signed up for weekly lessons. She was quite patient and understanding but, after six weeks or so, it became evident to me that it would take me about five years to play my first performance. During this disconcerting revelation, a fortuitous event occurred that was to have a significant effect on my entertainment future.

While attending a fundraiser for Ti-Ahwaga Players, a local community theater group, I bid on six guitar lessons and won lessons donated by a Canadian performer, Daphne Braden. I thought that $56 was a little steep but it was for a good cause. My next task was purchasing a decent guitar with the help of my son, Jeffrey, who had taken lessons as a teenager and was well versed on the subject. When he demonstrated a rosewood Taylor, I was sold. My weekly lessons began in earnest in Daphne's upstairs apartment. After the first six prepaid lessons, she asked if I wanted to continue at her normal rate. After I told her I would be interested, she asked what I planned to do with my newfound skill. "Perform a one-man comedy show," was my reply. She did not respond that I was the least funny student she was teaching. Instead, she said, "Would you like a partner?" I quickly jumped at the chance to team up with such a polished professional.

So, the musical duo of Orv Wright and Daphne Braden premiered at the Tioga Trails Café on August 28, 2003 to a sell out crowd paying $8.00 a ticket. By January of 2004, we hired the Ti-Ahwaga theatre, with a seating capacity of 150, to listen to "Protest, Sounds of the 60s." Several people in the audience thought we were actually protesting the Iraq War. (A graduate of the Naval Academy with a military career of 23 years would be an unlikely candidate to protest a war.) Our next theme, performed in August of 2004 was "The Difficulty of Growing Up in America." Again, there was a full house for the show. After paying Daphne half the profits, the remainder of each of the five performances went to various charities. "Love Songs for the Gullible" happened in April of 2005 followed by our final show in December of 2007, entitled "Another Evening with Orv Wright and Daphne Braden." This was a dinner show with tickets selling for $35, which 165 patrons paid. By the way, our piano tuner, Mike Mansfield and his wife Debbie, turned into our biggest fans during our run. Opinions at first sight are not always accurate.

At the same time, I contacted Tabor Children's Services (TCS), the organization that resulted when Tabor Home for Children went out of the business of institutional housing of needy children. They needed an instructor for résumé writing and job interviewing skills. I volunteered to conduct quarterly workshops on the two topics. The president of the board invited me to become a trustee and I accepted. It involved quarterly attendance at board meetings, supporting the organization financially, and giving advice on running TCS.

Fred Plequette, a former member of the Board of Trustees at TCS, had recorded an oral history of the 10 years he had lived at Tabor Home from 1922 until he graduated from high school in 1932. He delivered the tape to Arianna Burrows, Chief Development Officer, who was impressed and thought collecting the memories of past attendees could be published as a fundraiser for TCS. Two large hurdles remained for the project; who would edit the recollections and who would fund the publication of the book. I volunteered to take oral histories from each former resident, write their story and send it back to them for accuracy and tone. In addition, I would cover the up-front publishing costs with the assurance that there would be no purging of unpleasant or unflattering remembrances. I started the task by trying to convert Fred's tape into an interesting story. I was stymied and put the tape aside while waiting for inspiration. The next month I received a phone call from Fred's daughter. Fred had died and she wanted the tape to be played at his funeral. I quickly restarted and finished the task, sent back the tape and the created story, which was used as his eulogy. With 49 more memories to write and edit, I realized the enormity of this fundraiser.

The first decision was to title the book. Immediately, the phrase 'Twas A Hard Knock Life came to mind since all of the mini-authors would agree that being raised in a childrens' home or orphanage was not easy. The next decision was to divide the anthology into chapters by the decade i.e. the 1930s, 1940s, 1950s, 1960s, 70s & 80s. Sadly, several of the older authors died before seeing their stories published. Not all of the past alumni of the Home were enthused about sharing their memories. A few were downright hostile, declaring, "I don't want anything to do with Tabor Home or anyone associated with it." Others demurred with a comment like, "I know no matter what I say, you will write what you want to make Tabor look good." For the most part, past residents were willing to share their thoughts about institutional living at Tabor. I was assisted in the effort by Dotty Buckner, who had spent 16 years living at Tabor and possessed a remarkable memory for events that occurred many decades earlier. My wife, Carolyn, also contributed by ensuring the punctuation and grammar were correct.

Here is an example of one of the memories that the authors related: "Harry Clark regretted getting into an argument with one of the Lutheran Sisters and being booted out of the Home at age 16. He joined the Merchant Marine and met a girl in New York City just after World War II started. With his ship scheduled to sail, his girlfriend (later his wife) gave him an ultimatum that if he got on that ship, he could kiss her goodbye for good. Harry decided to go AWOL (Absent without leave). One week later his ship was sunk by a German U-boat and all hands were lost. "The best decision I ever made in my life," Harry declared. He concluded his story with these lines; "I was drafted into the Army and served three and one-half years until the war ended. If I had to live my life over again, I would choose to spend my childhood at Tabor Home. That is how much I appreciated the Home."

Another resident confided that he had a dark secret about an event he had experienced as a teenager and wondered whether it was wise to share it at this late date. I counseled him that I would run the story if he decided it was the right thing to do, but he should remember that, although the perpetrator had died, his relatives might read the book. After several days, he decided nothing positive would come of revealing the incident that occurred several decades ago.

The memory I contributed to the book was the 'sling shot' story described in Chapter Two. This unfortunate incident happened in 1947, when I was 13 years old. As I recalled the deed and published it in 2007, it never occurred to me that George Coulton might still be living and discover the secret of the ancient warriors who attacked him 60 years ago. But, later that year, I received a call from George wanting to purchase a copy of the book. I put him off by telling him I would get back to him and discussed the dilemma with my wife. Her position was that I could absolutely not charge him money for a copy. I quickly thought of my options; redact page 90 or perhaps just rip out that page and hope he would not notice, or send him a complimentary copy and face the music for my misdeed. In the end, I called George and convinced him I would send him a free copy and I wished him well. I am hoping he will not request a copy of *Drifting in the Wake*.

At publication time, the assurances that I had received about censoring the stories seemed to have been forgotten by Tabor staff members, since the draft copy I had submitted was edited by removing any references to unpleasant events which the authors had experienced. I met with the staff and strongly objected to their 'revising history' and told them the project was dead unless the original script was approved. The disagreement went to the board president, John Trainer, who, with just a few changes, ruled in my favor.

The back cover of *'Twas A Hard Knock Life* contained the following paragraph, "Tabor Home For Children was founded a century ago in Philadelphia but moved to Doylestown, PA in 1913. This remarkable anthology captures the memories and recollections of 50 of those residents spread over six decades. The experience of being raised in a childrens' home with 40 boys and 40 girls will enlighten, sadden, amuse and surprise most readers. The individual stories are told in a forthright style expressing remorse, gratitude, anger, joy, spirituality and excitement. The book is uplifting and depressing, adventurous and predictable, happy and sad, just like life itself." You can check it out on the web site, AHardKnockLife.com.

A major surprise occurred after the book was published. In June of 2007, I received a typed letter from Rosalind Case Avrett, a successful author and elementary classmate, who had won the 8th grade award in English.

"I really enjoyed Twas A Hard Knock Life. When I read page 88, I was in tears. I had <u>no</u> idea! Those wretched teachers. (But I really did win the 1946 Gross Award for the highest average in Bucks County.) Well, I hope 60 years isn't too late. All the best, and congratulations. Love, Roz." (Enclosed was the actual book Roz won entitled The Good Master. In addition there was a five dollar bill inside the cover.)

I sent her a thank you note and mentioned I was looking forward to seeing her at our next class reunion. Unfortunately, Roz passed away in 2008.

On October 12, 2007, I was fortunate to be elected into the Central Bucks High School Athletic Hall of Fame. It was based upon my record as a three-letter (football, basketball and baseball) man in high school, but particularly because in my senior year, I had broken the Bux-Mont League basketball scoring record by amassing 31 points against Ambler High School. I was also selected to the first team all-league basketball team. As nice as it was to be inducted in 2007, it was equally satisfying two years later, when my brother, Will, joined me as a posthumous member. In my induction speech for him, I highlighted that in military aviation, all gave some, but some gave all. Along with another Tabor graduate, Don Fritz, it spoke well that three of the 'Home kids' were honored as outstanding athletes. Only one other family of brothers, Tom and Ed Redfield, had been elected to the Hall.

My fifth retirement goal was to contribute to society in some meaningful way. A rather easy way was to join a service club whose purpose is to make the community and the world a better place. Looking into service clubs, our good friend, Martin Tillapaugh, strongly suggested the Owego Rotary Club, which met weekly at a local hotel and supported various charities, local, national, and international. They also had a student exchange program with the express intent of having teenagers exposed to foreign cultures. It seemed like a good fit, so we applied for membership shortly after returning from England.

Rotary International is a service organization that was founded in 1905 by Paul Harris, a Chicago lawyer, who was trying to start a social club among business owners. After it changed into a service club, the idea spread like wild fire both in this country and eventually world-wide. It now has over 35,000 clubs and 1.2 million members. Its motto is Service Above Self.

After joining, Carolyn and I were asked to assume duties as joint club secretaries. Carolyn stayed on for the next 18 years and counting, while I served as club president in 2005-2006 and subsequently filled various positions at the district level. Our first Rotary International convention in Chicago, in which 30,000 attendees experienced the huge impact that Rotarians had on the world, sold us on the importance of being part of improving people's lives. We have since attended conventions in Niagara Falls, Montreal, Toronto, New Orleans, and Atlanta. In 2007, I was elected to become Governor of District 7170 during the Rotary year of 2010-2011, quite an honor for a Tabor kid who was publicly described as a 'deadhead' by the elementary school principal. Opinions at first sight are not always accurate.

Tioga County AARP Foundation sponsors a Tax-Aide Program that prepares tax returns for senior citizens with moderate incomes at no cost to the recipient. They operate at four or five different sites with about nine IRS-certified tax counselors, working from January to April each year. I joined the organization 15 years ago and find it is a meaningful way to assist seniors at tax time. Clients are most grateful and it makes their life a little less stressful.

Over the years I have been asked to be Master of Ceremony (MC) at various functions such as going-away parties for Martin and Meg Tillapaugh and Laura Costello (Wood), as well as for Rotary District Foundation Dinners. I volunteered to give a talk entitled "Observations of a Navy Helicopter Test Pilot" as a fundraiser for the local Library's elevator fund. It was a donation-only affair and was given to a packed house although many in the audience attended, thinking it was going to be a comedy show. It raised $700 toward the Library's goal of 500,000 dollars.

The remaining task on my 'to-do' list was to ensure my children did not spend their retirement years in poverty by creating and annually funding a Roth IRA for each of the six children. It is still a work in progress, but it appears to be working. As several of my friends have remarked when learning of my plan, "Will you consider adopting us?"

So, as the ship of life continues its voyage and the wake becomes wider, I could not be more grateful for all that life has granted me; great friends, interesting shipmates, talented business acquaintances, marvelous Rotarians, athletic tennis and Pickle Ball players, loving family members and a wife that dreams are made of. Life has exceeded all expectations and no man could ask for more!

CHAPTER **17**

Reflections on Life

No one is in charge of your happiness but you.

GROWING OLD HAS a number of advantages that are generally understated in our youth-oriented society. One comes to grips with status. You know you will never be President of the United States, or Governor of New York State, or be selected the sexiest man in Hollywood by People Magazine. What's more, it doesn't matter to you. If you reach your eighth decade and haven't figured life out, you get low marks for attention to detail. On the other hand, I don't want to be too critical of anyone who has slogged through sixteen chapters of someone else's life and is still reading. So, as Woody Allen replied when asked how he evaluates blind dates, "If they show up, I give them a passing grade." Congratulations on getting to the last chapter! Thanks for showing up.

During my retirement years, I conducted several non scientific polls, asking the following questions. "Of all the people you know, what percentage would answer yes to this statement? Life is hard."

Answers ran the gamut from five to 100 percent. The younger the respondent, the higher the number was. Many, including every social worker asked, responded with percentages exceeding 95. The average number was in the 75-80 range. A number of married couples varied up to 50 percent between themselves with their answers.

Several stated that they would answer the question about what percentage would answer yes, but that many who thought their life was hard did not actually have a hard life.

I am not an admirer of commencement addresses anymore than taking advice on careers from successful people. That said, occasionally some remarks make so much sense that you want to stand and shout, "Listen, young people and heed." Such words were spoken by Chief Justice of the Supreme Court, John Roberts at his son's graduation.

"From time to time in the years to come, I hope you will be treated unfairly, so you will come to know the value of justice. I hope you will suffer betrayal because that will teach you the importance of loyalty. Sorry to say, but I hope you will be lonely from time to time so that you don't take friends for granted. I wish you bad luck so that you will be conscious of the role of chance in life and understand that your success is not completely deserved and the failure of others is not completely deserved either. And, when you lose, as you will from time to time, I hope every now and then, your opponent will gloat over your failure. It is a way for you to understand the importance of sportsmanship. I hope you will be ignored so you know the importance of listening to others, and I hope you have just enough pain to learn compassion. Whether I wish these things or not, they're going to happen. And whether you benefit from them or not will depend on your ability to see the message in your misfortune."

Being treated unfairly was commonplace growing up at Tabor Home so all Tabor kids knew the value of justice. The importance of loyalty was foremost in my value system along with the 40 boys and 40 girls that experienced the same institutional rearing. Every child was lonely and felt unloved but we all learned to 'suck it up' early in life. I never understood the role that chance played in my life so I tended to take credit when the breaks came my way. It was much later that I came to understand the randomness of good fortune and that it would not last forever. Every athlete gets to experience loss and the gloating of opponents. As my father used to say, "If two people

193

ride on a horse, one has to ride behind. Get used to it." I do think that I benefited from a hard childhood. And I treated plebe year and survivor training like a drama that had a plot, a cast of characters, a crisis or two but in the end everything would turn out all right. I certainly learned the value of tenacity in coping with challenges! Thankfully my misfortunes were few and never life threatening, unlike some of my colleagues.

Life expectancy in the United States for a white male who reaches 65 is, as I write this last chapter, 85 years. Projections, based on my lifestyle, indicate I shall live until 91. I am already playing with house money. My Dad died at age 88, but had told all his friends and acquaintances that he was 10 years younger than he was. At his funeral, a number of attendees asked how old he was. I didn't know what to say, so I changed the subject.

What exactly have I learned in the past 80 years or so? Here are some findings in no special order.

- A man is not old as long as he has intelligence and affection.
- Those of us who have been successful in both investing and marriage tend to think of ourselves as geniuses. We forget the big part chance or luck played.
- You cannot reason a man out of a position he has not reasoned himself into.
- Logic wins out, progress happens, and problems have solutions.
- Never, ever, add to a losing position in the stock market (i.e. average down)
- Don't be yourself; be someone nicer.
- Being born smart gives one a tremendous advantage in life, but dogged determination is a better attribute to possess in predicting success.
- Never miss an opportunity to make others happy, even if you have to leave them in order to do it.
- Accept the hand you're dealt with grace, and play it as well as you can.

- Examples and stories are the most effective means for teaching any subject.
- You cannot do a kindness too soon, for you never know how soon it will be too late.
- Problem solving ability is a better indicator of intelligence than scoring high on an IQ test.
- Give advice, not criticism.
- Spend your time with positive, cheerful, and optimistic people.
- See the humor in life. Laugh a lot.
- Laughing at your own mistakes lengthens your life; laughing at your wife's mistakes shortens it.
- It is very easy to spot a boring person. He or she will never ask a single question about you.
- A smile is an inexpensive way to improve your looks.
- A person who has had an insecure childhood will admit to a failure within the first five minutes, such as "I failed the 3rd grade." (This seemingly protects him or her from criticism.)
- Every person has two characteristics; personality and character. We are overly impressed with a sparkling personality. If you plan to have a relationship with someone, please choose the one with solid character.
- Bad decisions make good stories.
- Advice to women; whatever you look like, marry a man your own age. As your looks fade, so will his eyesight.
- High achievers tend to be first-born or only children. They come from predominantly middle class homes.
- There is no link between talent and family wealth.
- Being tall gives you an extraordinary advantage in life.
- Two secrets to keep your marriage a success;
    1. Whenever you're wrong, admit it.
    2. Whenever you're right, shut up!
- If a woman says "Do what you want!" Do **not** do what you want. Stand still. Do not blink. Don't even breathe. Just play dead!

- The biggest lie I tell myself, "I don't need to write that down. I'll remember it."
- Light travels faster than sound. This is why some people appear bright until you hear them speak.
- It is easier to get older than it is to get wiser.
- The first testicular cup was used in hockey in 1874 and the first hockey helmet was used in 1974. That means it took 100 years for men to realize their brain is also important.
- We need to question our assumption that youth is the best time in life and everything after it is worse.
- Arguing with your wife is like reading the Software License Agreement. In the end, you ignore everything and click, "I agree."
- You can tell a lot about a woman's mood by her hands. If they are holding a gun, she's probably quite angry!
- Never take a sleeping pill and a laxative on the same night.
- The big lie indeed is that 'It is sweet and fitting to die for one's country.'
- You can grow older, just don't grow old.
- Old is good in some things ...old songs ...old movies, and best of all, old friends.

As life progresses, I hope to add to the list of things I have learned, but to predict how long that will be, is anyone's guess. Wake up each week and proclaim, "Monday morning, and another week in which to excel."

Index

Brown, Helen, 36
Buckner, Dotty, 126, 187
Burke, Joe, 109
Burmeister, Harry "Boog," 13, 14
Burnett, Bill, 123
Burns, Ken, 60
Burrows, Arianna, 186

C
Cain, Bill, 136
Caine, Nancy, 136
Caine, Paul, 135–136, 139
Cameron, Sam, 154
Carius, Robert W., 142, 143
Carnevale, Ben, 47
Carr, Gerald, 144
Carrier Anti-Submarine Air
  Group 59, 134, 137
Case, Rosalind. *See* Avrett,
  Rosalind Case
Central Bucks High School
  Hall of Fame of, 189
  OW's memorial to Wilbur at,
    128–129
  Wilbur at, 33, 47, 51
  see also Doylestown High
    School
Chaddock, Paul, 35
Chesney, Ed, 34
Chidester, Emma, 5
Ching, Chew Chong, 68
Chiocchio, Stan, 117, 129
Clark, Harry, 187
Cohen, Mickey, 147

Cohn, Len, 161
Connell, Jack, 117, 120
Corbett, Bob, 117
Corprew, Gerard, 165
Coulton, Bruce, 15
Coulton, George, 15, 16,
  187–188
Cox, Allan, 151
"crashing," term not used by
  aviators, 80, 106
Crossfield, Scott, 166

D
Darling, Al, 109
Dauber, Lenny, 24
Davidson, Adam (son-in-law),
  164–165
Davidson, Nanette Louise
  Wright (daughter), 112, 123,
  130–131, 164, 165
defense contractors
  OW's presentation to mid-
    shipmen and, 132
  TPS and, 111
  see also IBM Federal Systems
    Division, Owego, NY;
    Sikorsky Aircraft Company;
    Westland Helicopter
    Limited
Defense Department, common
  designator codes for aircraft,
  90, 99
Denney, Ron, 54
DeVries, Bucky, 79, 147

CPSIA information can be obtained
at www.ICGtesting.com
Printed in the USA
FFHW021923160919
55040800-60731FF

9 780578 220833